FROM VICTIM TO VICTORIOUS

~The Testimony~

BY

MARJORIE SIMON

From Victim to Victorious by Marjorie Simon

Copyright © 2004

ISBN#: 0-9715603-1-5

Library of Congress Card # Pending

Additional copies of this book are available by mail. Send $12.00 each (includes tax and postage) to:

Don E. Simon
The Storm is Over Publishing
P.O. Box 311552
Atlanta, Georgia 31131

For Booking Information or Book Signing Engagements Call:

(404) 629-6595

~Biography~

Born March 25, 1943 in Ellaville, Georgia. Marjorie graduated from high school in 1961 and moved to Atlanta, Georgia where she worked as a live-in maid for approximately four months. She later left Atlanta, Georgia and moved to Rochester, New York and worked for a Travel Lodge Hotel where she cleaned rooms for a short time. Marjorie then moved to Syracuse, New York, where she lived for 33 years. She worked for General Electric Company for 6 years, drove a taxi for 5 years and worked for Miller Brewing Company for 18 years. Currently, Marjorie resides in the Cascades of Atlanta, Georgia where she is prosperous and living the good life.

~Dedication~

This book is dedicated to my five children:

Wardell Simon, Jr.
Laurie A. Simon
Dolores M. Simon-Burgess
Don E. Simon
Ronda R. Darity

And to my seven grandchildren:

Theodore Simon
Jauquin Booker
Jameel Simon
Kharia Burgess
Jaylin Darity
Emaui Burgess
Jalissa Darity

This book was written in loving memory of my dear mother and father. I praise God for my mama. She was one of my best friends and we had a special bond with one another. My mother thought I could do anything because she realized my faith walk with God. My father was a great provider for us and I loved them both dearly.

~ACKNOWLEDGMENTS~

First, I give all the glory and honor to my Lord and Savior Jesus Christ for sparing my life and giving me strength to make it through these storms. If it had not been for the grace of God, I would not be here. I dedicate my life to Him forever!

I would like to give special honor to my younger son Don for encouraging me to write this book. He was the one that motivated me and had confidence that I could do this. He encouraged me to keep writing. I am grateful for the inspiration I gained from him. His wisdom and knowledge pushed me to go forward. I just want to give a special thanks to you, Don.

I would like to acknowledge the ministries that have impacted my life. I was born again while attending Gospel Temple Church of God in Christ in Syracuse, New York, under the leadership of the late Dr. Heard Seals. I was a member for 28 years and served on the Board of Trustees.

After moving to Atlanta, Georgia, I joined World Changers Church International (WCCI) under the ministry leadership of Dr. Creflo A. Dollar, Jr. I served as a counselor for the outreach department, Project Change, as well as a greeter in which I still work in that capacity. While serving in the ministries, I maximized the ministry gifts that were already within me by graduating from a two-year program at the WCCI School of Ministry.

~Author's Words~

This book is based on my true testimony and is dedicated to hurting women and men that may have gone through a divorce or separation and may have children on drugs and all kinds of problems. It is designed to bring deliverance and victory in every area of one's life. This book is not to condemn or criticize; it just happens to be the true facts about my life. I would like to share how I came out victorious in some of the same areas that you may be going through now. I want you to know that all things are possible with God. I have been there and I know if you put your trust in Him, He will bring you out all right. May God bless the words in this book so that they may penetrate into your heart. I believe they will lift you up and give you courage to go through, no matter what storm you might be in now. No matter what it may look like it is not over until it is over. My friends, I encourage you to hang in there, you must know that precious things cost much but they are worth it. Bishop T.D. Jakes once said, "The storm does not have to move, but if you just keep walking you will walk through it!" So get ready to take this journey with me as I share some of the storms I have walked through.

As you read this book, it may make you laugh, or even cry, but I pray that it will bring peace and tranquility into your life. I hope that after you read this book that your life will never be the same again. I pray that it will let you know that whatever you may be going through–the storm will pass, not last!

God bless you,
Marjorie Simon

~PROLOGUE~

Now that I am no longer a victin, but victorious, you can read and see how I overcame every storm. I was born on a farm and grew up under some hard times. I fell in love at a young age, to the man of my dreams who I loved with my whole heart and then I lost him. It was very devastating for me but I overcame it. I went on with my life and moved to New York and began to look for love, but in all the wrong places and with too many faces. I met a man that I thought could ease my pain, and after a short love life, we married and began to have children. One of my dreams was to be a wonderful mother and wife. I thought I had finally arrived but after four years of marriage it seemed that all hell had broken loose. I realized that this dream had not come true, however, I was determined to stay in it. With much heartache and pain, it made me wonder, "Is this all there is in life to gain?" But after seventeen years of a bad marriage, I was left alone with five children and no child support from my husband.

After all the children had graduated from high school and some went on to college, I thought this was the time for me to relax and take it easy to do some of the things I did not have time to do while raising them. My children were very special to me and they always came first in my life. I always said they did not ask to come here, so they were my responsibility. God blessed me with a good paying job, and I was able to give my children the best of everything. I worked at my job for eighteen years, a job in which I thought I would retire with a good pension and do some traveling, but life had been full of surprises for me.

After my last child graduated from high school and attended two years of college, another storm came. My job closed down after eighteen years, leaving me without any benefits and very little money. Yet I thought there was still hope. I knew my father had over two hundred acres of land, and there were only three girls in the family. My brother had died earlier in life, so I thought my father would do the right thing by leaving the land equally to his three daughters.

My father had known all the struggles I had in my marriage, the struggles of raising my children alone. I never asked my father for any assistance while these struggles took place. Now my job was gone and I was ready to make a major decision to leave New York and move back home to Georgia. Shortly before I moved back, I found out that in my father's last will and testament, he had given almost all of his land to my two sisters and only left me with 9.1 acres. In the will, he would give one of my sisters 135 acres and the other sister the home and the rest of the land. At the point of losing my job, I did not know what to do. I had a son that lived in Atlanta, who had graduated from college. He told me to come and stay with him, so I did.

After getting to Atlanta, two of my daughters and a grandson were already living with my son. He had a two-bedroom apartment, but was willing to make a sacrifice for his family. When I arrived, I felt like I was in a wilderness. I felt that everything I had dreamed of, had worked for, and believed God for, was closing in on me! I had left my seven-room home in New York because I had no job to take care of the expenses. Now I was in my son's two-bedroom apartment sleeping on the floor. Well, how do you think I felt? I felt as if life had dealt me a bad hand, but I knew that God would not allow me to be tested, if He did not know I would pass the test.

One day, I began to look at all that had happened to me and I began to cry out to the Lord saying, "Lord, I just do not understand." I could not understand why my marriage did not work out, why my job closed down, why my father had treated me so unfairly with his land. As I was crying, pouring my heart out to God telling Him I did not understand, I heard the voice of God say to me, "My child, I have a plan." He said, "I will not leave you empty-handed," and even after that, I still did not understand. All I knew was that I had to trust Him.

Things went on for a while; a lot of things I still did not understand, and I even questioned God about some of the things that were happening around me. All I could hear in a soft still voice was "Trust Me." When it seems like all hope is gone, I can tell you how God gave me strength to carry on.

Sleeping on the floor for three years, I did not complain, because I knew I had heard from God and He was not going to leave me there.

"Now that I'm victorious and no longer a victim", I can say that God has truly blessed me unspeakably. He blessed me to get off the floor and move into a new home worth $295,000 paid in full with cash. Now I can tell you how I weathered my storms and came out victorious and prosperous. It was not easy, but it was worth it. Now I live in peace and prosperity. I am living the good life...the storms may come, but they will not overcome in any area of my life!

TABLE OF CONTENTS

CHAPTER ONE

A Young Dreamer

I was a small-town girl with a big-city dream. It all began in the town of Ellaville, Georgia, population 1,600. Ellaville's claim to fame is its close proximity to Plains, Georgia, the home of former President Jimmy Carter. Once you've traveled about five miles outside of Ellaville, you will come to that dirt road that led to my parents' farm. There were no neighbors within miles of our farm, other than my grandparents. We had every imaginable animal you would find on a farm: cows, hogs, mules and chickens; at least it seemed that way through my eyes. I assume most kids would have been excited about picking cotton, slopping hogs or feeding chickens, however, for me I never got used to the idea. Ellaville's excitement back in those days was going to town on Saturday and the old folks sitting around the park in the center of town swapping stories, while we youngsters had an opportunity to see our friends from school. I couldn't wait for Saturday to come!

To say the least, I had a very humble beginning: no streetlights, electricity, hot water, inside toilets, nor running water, just an old-fashioned water pump. Have you ever tried walking down an old country road at night with no streetlights? You can barely see your hand even if it was directly in your face, but the beauty of the night stars is beyond description. I guess I was like most little girls at the age of 13, except for my height, needing the love and nurturing of their parents as well as the companionship of their siblings. Each day as my school bus slowed to a stop at the end of that dirt road, it was like turning back the hand of time, because at school there was electricity, running water and many amenities that most took for granted.

I was born on March 25th, 1943, to proud parents, Napoleon and Rosa Alridge. I was the third of four children, three girls and one boy. As I think back I can remember the smell of mother's biscuits filling the house early every morning although it was the alarm clock that woke us up each morning. She was known throughout Ellaville as a wonderful cook and a devoted housewife. No one could beat mother baking cakes and pies as far as I'm concerned. My memories of her were seeing her provide for our family and I knew I could always depend on her for that. Many days I just stared as she went through her routine, asking the question in my mind, where does she find the energy? The mindset of a child is expecting our parents to love us. For that we, as children, seldom say thank you.

My father was a very proud man whom the community respected because of his success and the way that he carried himself. I used to wonder why he was so proud of this farm; I believe that because so many black families didn't have the opportunity to own their own homes he felt a certain sense of accomplishment, because we would always have a place we could call home. I couldn't really appreciate his view of things simply because I didn't understand the struggles many blacks went through back in the 40's and 50's. He worked constantly as a self-employed trucker. Some days I wouldn't even see him because his day began before we woke for school and ended after mother had put us to bed. He even provided hauling services for the Carter family (former President Jimmy Carter) in Plains, Georgia. He had also acquired over two hundred acres of land. He was the consummate provider of our daily needs, however, I realized that I would need more from him than he was able to give me on his own. In those days most men and women were taught to earn an honest living, and meet the demands of their homes.

For some unknown reason I became more attached to my brother. I felt a need to protect him as well as my sisters. Back then I was tall for my age and was always ready to defend my family. But, there was a shy and innocent person that was still waiting to blossom on the inside. My brother and I spent many hours playing marbles, climbing trees and anything else that made us happy on the farm. Even when one of us was given a chore usually we would try and help the other so that we wouldn't have to do it alone. I have so much love for my brother even though he was five years older than I was. If you tried to hurt him, you had to come through me first. As I reflect back on my life I may have tried to substitute the male affirmation I needed from my father with the male affirmation of my brother.

My parents were married for sixty years. Maybe that's where I got this notion that marriage can last forever. At 13 I began to dream of my future and where I might end up. Of one thing I was sure: I wouldn't end up in Ellaville. What prompted me to leave Ellaville was the thought of me seeing more of the world. After my brother had planned to move away, I realize that I would be losing my best friend and confidant. How could I survive without him? It's amazing how child-like faith empowers the will of a man and can safely thrust him/her through some of the most difficult times in our lives.

That same year my brother did move to Florida with my aunt and uncle. I was miserable without him; we didn't have a telephone so I had to patiently wait on his letters. I guess what made me miss him so much is that he was the first to leave home and he was my only brother, so it's a natural response for a little sister to miss her brother. Eventually he started dating a young lady, and soon after they got married. I finally realized that I had to accept the fact that he had become a man and now had a family of his own.

My father was very strict, so we didn't have many friends other than the young girls we worked with in the fields each day after school. It felt as though I was on an island with no other civilization within miles until one day I met the love of my life, what some may refer to as their soul mate. It seemed like the sun rose upon him. He was good looking! He was from a well-respected family and my father and his father were very good friends. We started writing love letters until we had a chance to get to know each other. He was sixteen, I was thirteen, but that didn't seem to matter much. For me it was love at first sight. The only time we could see each other was at school or Saturday uptown where the country folks would gather together. Even though I wasn't crazy about school I never wanted to miss a day because I wanted to see my boyfriend. We officially started dating a few weeks after we met. Our mothers were a little less strict than our fathers and would talk to us about our relationship. His mother really cared for me. She even suggested to him that I might be his wife one day.

But as time moved on he started working in the summer with the seasonal workers who would leave Ellaville at the beginning of the summer and return at the end of the summer. That was a very difficult time for us both because we were not accustomed to not seeing each other each week. However, I understood that's what most young men in Ellaville did to earn money in the summer. After three years of dating I ended up losing my virginity to him. In those days I didn't realize the importance of abstinence and how physical intimacy was intended for a husband and wife. All I knew then was that I loved him and he loved me and that was all that mattered to me (one thing I can say now is that I am glad that my father cannot read this book, because as strict as he was he would want to beat my butt even now).

In the eleventh grade I seemed to open up a little more, I got involved in basketball because of the encouragement of my principal. To my surprise I was pretty good at it. Spending so much time with my brother must have developed an interest in sports. Life seemed to be getting a little better on the farm until the summer of my eleventh grade year when my boyfriend didn't return with the seasonal workers as he had in the past. I didn't know what to think, Christmas was soon approaching and still there was no word from him. I started thinking the worst—maybe he found someone else. Facing the terrible fact that he was not coming back, I became a little impatient and upset.

Christmas came and, as you can imagine, his absence didn't make the heart grow fonder. I finally gave in to loneliness and pity, agreeing to go on a double date with my sister, hoping it would fill the void. Sometimes in life we have to trust the voice of this young dreamer that lives inside. I knew that what I saw in his eyes was real, but I allowed doubt to convince me that I was being a fool if I waited. As fate would have it, the same night of the date he returned to surprise me. When I came home that night, the first thing my mother said to me was, "Your first love is back in town, and he has been here looking for you." She said, "He seems to be very upset that you were not home." He promised to return the next day to see me, which he did. Have you ever met someone that when you looked into their eyes your spirit leaped, or you couldn't stop smiling? That's the effect he had on me.

At the time, I was too young to understand what being spiritually yoked with a person really meant. It's more than infatuation or lust, it involves being completely vulnerable and trusting because everything is completely exposed spiritually.

Because of the confusion and hurt, there were very few words that we exchanged during our meeting. How was I supposed to know that he would come back? Deep down inside I wanted to tell him how much I missed him, but there was a part of me that was angry because he hadn't said a word for so long. Basically our flesh and pride got in the way. I knew he was very disappointed in me for seeing someone else, but what I did not know is that someone had lied to him about me and told him things about me that hurt him. He didn't stay around to see if it was true or not. He said, " I am leaving this town for good," and he did.

I couldn't wait for the day to come for me to graduate so I could leave Ellaville behind me. He never kept in touch with me anymore, but his mother would let me know how he was doing, she really loved me as a daughter. I heard through his family that he moved to another town and met someone else. Before I could graduate I discovered he was going to be a father. I tried to convince myself I didn't care, but when I heard he was getting married, I realized my dream for him was over. Why do we so easily give up on our dreams? I think mostly it's the fear of them never coming true. Well, if we stop believing and cease to pursue them, how will we ever know? So, part of the dreamer inside me died when he left, because I believed that the dream died. I knew it was time for me to move on with my life, although it was very difficult knowing that the man that I had loved from the age of thirteen would no longer be in my life.

After many sleepless nights and tears, I began to think about my future and the many possibilities that life offered. So, when I graduated from high school, I left the small town of Ellaville, Georgia the next week and moved to the big city, Atlanta, Georgia. Can you imagine a small town girl like me in Atlanta, Georgia? Compared to Ellaville, it was like night and day. God was so gracious, the very same day I arrived in Atlanta, I got a job as a live in housekeeper. In those days that's what most black women in the south did to earn a living. I was only eighteen years old working as a maid, taking care of a family of six: a husband, a wife and four children. I was responsible for maintaining all of the domestic affairs of the home for only $25 a week. It didn't take me long to realize that this was not what I was going to do for the rest of my life.

I knew that God had something greater for me if I had the ability to believe and trust him for it. So, I decided to leave Atlanta and explore what seemed to be

9

greener pastures, with my uncle in Rochester, New York. I knew that better job opportunities awaited me, but I was also seeking refuge, trying to get over losing the man that I loved.

As you read this book and discover the many events that shaped my life, you'll begin to see and understand this young dreamer named Marjorie Simon, who always knew that somehow, someway, someone was watching and cared enough to grant me strength and grace to endure the heartaches and disappointments of life. Who would have known that these life experiences are more than just storms, they're life lessons that draw us closer to God? I understood that my beginnings were very small, but God promised that my latter end would be greatly increased (Job 8:7).

CHAPTER TWO

Searching For Peace

After leaving Ellaville and making a short stop in Atlanta, I ended up in Rochester, New York, a place known for its brutal winters. I moved in with my family (uncle and aunt) so that I could have time to get settled and find a place of my own. Even though I was excited about leaving Ellaville, there was a part of me that missed my parents, sisters and brother. Even though my sisters and I didn't spend much time together growing up, I longed for their acceptance and support. When I arrived in Rochester, I began to reflect on my childhood and how I couldn't remember the embrace of my father, nor girl talks with my mother. I pretended that those things really weren't important, but as I grew older I realized how significant they were to this young dreamer in an adult body. Though I was thousands of miles from Ellaville, my heart was still held captive by the love of my life.

After living in Rochester for about six months things seemed to go downhill. Loneliness and depression set in and the answer to my dilemma was nowhere in sight. I was having a hard time trying to adjust and nothing seemed to be working in my favor. I started trying to make sense out of the confusion, with no success. You know how sometimes in life we try putting bandages on wounds that require surgery. I guess that's what I was doing in my attempt to alleviate the pain.

One night there was a concert in town, the Ike and Tina Turner Show. Being a small town girl from Ellaville, I had never been to a major event such as this. With no boyfriend I decided to attend the concert alone. The lights, staging and thousands of fans screaming was an experience I'll never forget. I was standing in the midst of all the excitement and still not enjoying the concert. I'm assuming it was because my heart was broken and I was still trying to avoid it.

I looked out over a sea of people, and I didn't know anyone there. Then I noticed a man across the arena starring at me from a distance. At first I thought he couldn't be looking at me, but after a short time he made it obvious by establishing eye contact. Slowly, he began working his way across the room. I'm thinking what does he want, what will he say? Finally he came over to where I was standing and introduced himself to me, asked if I was alone, and if I would be interested in a dance. We danced for hours it seemed; however, the concert was coming to an end. He got up the nerve to ask if I was married, I said no, then he asked for my telephone number. He said he lived in Syracuse, New York, which was about seventy miles from Rochester. So, I figured why not give him my number, not expecting him to call. He was a perfect gentleman and got my coat then we said goodbye. He said, "I will call you, if you do not mind." Sure enough, the next day he called and asked me if he could come to Rochester to see me. Well, that blew my mind to think that he wanted to drive seventy miles to see me; he must have really wanted to be with me, so I agreed.

During his trip to Rochester I asked him questions about his past and he was honest. Many of the things he shared weren't necessarily what I wanted or was prepared to hear. He stated that he was currently separated from his wife for three years and also had children from the marriage. He was contemplating filing for divorce due to acts of adultery committed by his wife. Yet he was still married! Shortly after our first meeting in Rochester we started dating. Things were looking up, I finally found someone who cared and would be there for me when I needed him. We dated for a while long distance before things got worse at home with my family in Rochester. At this time, I knew that I had to leave.

With no other family in the area I considered moving closer to my new love. Knowing that shacking (living together) was not an option, my boyfriend suggested that I move in with his friends until his divorce was final. Within a year the divorce proceedings were complete. As I think back I never considered the lifelong impact of the choice that I was about to make. There are times in the life of a young girl, I feel you need the counsel and input of a God-fearing mother. So, I made the decision to get married. The details of my wedding day are still blurred. Most say it should be the most memorable day of a girl's life, but for me something was missing. Shortly after our marriage I was pregnant with my first child.

The happiness I experienced giving birth to my first-born, Wardell, Jr. is unexplainable. As women we possess the ability to manifest the ultimate expression of love through child bearing. At that moment, when I gave birth, I realized that I was given the responsibility to

13

care for human life and provide the tools that I needed as a child. What an awesome stewardship! Giving birth was a miracle within itself, after being diagnosed as a child with a severe navel hernia, which gave me many problems even as a child, having a seven-pound baby boy was simply a blessing. The doctor told my mother that the older I got it would get worse and he recommended that I have surgery by the age of twelve. But God worked a miracle; I never went through with the operation.

The doctor stated that if I attempted to have children, most likely I wouldn't be able to carry the baby full term, plus I may have major complications during the birth. Not only did I carry Wardell, Jr. full term, but the remaining four children as well. Doctors know some things but God knows all things. God can do anything but fail!

Thank God for being in control of my life. It seemed that the pieces of the puzzle were finally coming together. I was happy to be married and to be a mother. Two years later I gave birth to my second child, a beautiful little girl, Laurie. We had a two-bedroom apartment and we were doing well. I had a good job working with General Electric and my husband was working for Carrier Air Conditioning, so I thought things were working out very well.

I always wanted to get married and have children and live happily ever after. That seems to be the dream of most young girls. Well, guess what? Real life doesn't work that way all of the time. Life sometimes presents challenges that make us stronger, however, they don't seem pleasant at the time. By now my husband and I had been married for a while. The honeymoon was over and getting acquainted with each other was, too. Now that we had two children, I noticed that my husband was becoming very impatient. He always drank, but he began to drink more and wouldn't come home after a day's work. His shift would end at 4:00 p.m., but he wouldn't get home until 8:00 p.m. at night. He began developing a habit of going straight from work to the bar. By the time he arrived home he didn't want to talk to me about anything. If I asked him where he had been, he would really get angry and start slapping me around. You might ask why did I put up with it? Deep in my heart I knew that he couldn't control the temptation.

During this dark period of our marriage I learned that he couldn't deal with much pressure, although he didn't seem too concerned about the pressure I was experiencing working, raising the children, and taking care of the affairs of our household. We didn't communicate very much unless we were arguing. He was away from us a lot and when he was not working, he just had to be in the streets. To avoid slipping back into depression and loneliness, I tried to keep myself busy with work and taking care of the children. The situation escalated to the point where he would leave home and would not come back until late in the evening or the next day. I can remember one night I was pacing the floor and looking out of the window wondering where my husband was and if he was all right. He never called home when he stayed out all night. I would ask him to please call me if he wasn't going to come home so that I would not worry all night. He asked me why should he have to call me. He said if anything happened to him, I would be the first one they would notify. It's amazing how love is blind to the offense, but is always seeking a way to heal or help.

One summer my sister-in-law, Vera (my husband's sister), was visiting with us. He was out late that night and I was upset, but yet worried about him. At this time I did not know how to trust God. I knew he drank heavily and gambled and had a quick temper. All I could think about was that someone had hurt him (you know when you do not know God as your personal Savior, the devil will make you think the worst things first). The later it got, the more I became a nervous wreck worrying about him. I went to the bedroom where my sister-in-law was sleeping, I woke her up crying, telling her I was afraid her brother was in some kind of trouble. By her being a mighty woman of God, she began ministering to me with loving kindness and told me I needed to put my trust in God and let God take care of my husband. She said, "You need the peace that only God can give." She began to talk to me about the goodness of God and how much He loved me and if I would just surrender my heart to Him, He would give me the peace I would need in the midst of this storm. After talking with her, I was able to go to bed and sleep.

The very next week we were having a revival at the church where I attended occasionally. Vera asked me to attend the revival with her. I didn't go because I really wanted to, but because she had shown me so much love and I felt obligated to go with her. I felt I was not ready to make a commitment to God, to be honest, I didn't understand what it meant to be totally committed. All I knew was that my life was in chaos, and I sought a peace that until now, I hadn't found. I made the same statement that so many others have made, when I get things together then I'll go to God. What I didn't know was that God loved me just as I was, and was seeking to grant me the peace I so desperately sought after. In reality it was a loving Father reaching out to a hurting little girl in her time of need. You see I had been everything to my husband and two children. My oldest child was two years and five months and my baby was only eight months. Out of all the things I was doing, there was still a void in my life. It dawned on me that the same nurture and love that I had desired for my children to experience, my heavenly father was offering me the same and more.

The first night of the revival, I went, but I sat there clinging to my baby, listening to the preacher talking about the love of God. When he finished, he asked if anyone wanted to come to the altar and give his or her life to God. My heart started pounding fast and I clung to my baby even tighter. My sister-in-law was watching me and she said, "Honey don't you want to go down to the altar for prayer?" I said, "No, I have my baby." So, she reached over and took the baby from me and she said, "It won't hurt you to go down just for prayer." Out of obedience I went to the altar, and that night, I felt the presence of the Almighty God. It was a love that no man could explain. I came away from the altar that night with God's peace in my heart; a peace that passes all understanding, a peace even in the midst of a storm. The next night of the revival she didn't have to tell me to go to the altar, I went by myself. God saved me and filled me with His precious Holy Spirit. And even though my marriage was falling apart, I had peace in knowing that I was not alone. That gave me joy unspeakable because Jesus Christ was in my life. After that night, my life has never been the same.

CHAPTER THREE

The Marriage Storm

After beginning my new life in Christ I assumed that I would never have to endure some of the experiences that I faced in the past. However, I found that God never said we wouldn't have to go in the fire, He simply promised to be with us and that He would never forsake us. That's a big difference from never having to face mountains in our lives. In any relationship it requires mutual adoration and affection for the other person. Even in my relationship with God, He never forced me to love Him or serve Him, but by His love drew me to Him and because of His sovereignty, I serve Him. Our natural relationships should be established upon the same mutual agape love.

The more I learned about the Lord the more I desired for my family to be whole and that our children be raised in a loving home where both parents were present. I didn't believe that what I hoped for was so far fetched; if we both tried I knew it was possible. By this time I was pregnant with our third child, Dolores, another beautiful little girl. I thought things were going to work out because my husband seemed to have snapped out of the nightmare he had been living in for the first two years of our marriage. He decided that it was time for me to stop working and raise the kids, which I thought was a noble idea. He got a part-time job in addition to his full-time employment. He started driving taxicabs part time, but little did I know; that this was the beginning of one of the major downfalls of our marriage!

The children and I seldom got a chance to see him. The children would be in bed by the time he came home and he would be gone to his full-time job by the time they got up, sounds familiar (home on the farm). By the time our third child was eight months old, I was pregnant again with the fourth child, a fine baby boy, Don. When Don was born, I knew our marriage was in serious trouble. My husband relapsed and started drinking and gambling, losing money more frequently. So when Don was old enough, I knew that I was going to have to go back to work. I wanted to help my husband; it hurt me so much to see him battling this addiction. Things were getting so far behind, but I didn't know what exactly to do to support him with four children. So, I decided to apply for a driver's permit to operate a taxicab five hours a day to help.

Fortunately, the two older children were in school all day. I figured if I could help my husband by driving part-time, maybe things would get better. However, when I went to work nothing changed. Maybe it wasn't just the financial woes that crippled our marriage, I believe it was the spiritual separation between us. Even through all the things my husband suffered he never sought the Lord for help. I was still a babe in Christ and really didn't know how to share my faith.

I knew that marriage was honorable, and God had gifted man with every tool to heal his marriage instead of divorce. However, God does not force a man to love. I was determined to make my marriage work, no matter what it took. Well, guess what? It takes two people working together to make a marriage work, and at that time I was the only one willing to work at it. I did not want to give up, but things got worse.

One Sunday evening I was sitting at home watching television when the phone rang. I answered the phone and said hello, it was a woman's voice on the other end. She asked to speak to my husband, naturally I responded, yes, who's calling? I could have never imagined the words that would come from her mouth next. She said to me, "I am the woman that your husband has been sleeping with" (not in those exact words) then she hung up the phone. Little to my surprise this was the beginning of a long harassment trip from this unknown woman. When I told my husband what this woman said to me, he didn't say a word, just got in his car and left. After about an hour, she showed up at our house, using unmentionable curse words loud enough for our neighbors to hear. How embarrassing this was to me. She knew that I wasn't a violent woman because my husband had told her all about me. When he came back home around midnight, I asked him was it true what this woman said. He said he didn't have to answer to me, because I was not his mammy. Can you imagine the hurt, finding out your husband was cheating on you and he seemed not to care that you found out? Although there had been many signs of unfaithfulness, in the back of my mind I didn't want to believe it. I guess what really bothered me was his attitude about the entire situation.

When you don't want to face the truth, you'll ignore all of the warning signs. What in life can ever prepare you for something like this? All I knew was to put my trust in God, believing that He would put no more on me than I could bear. My heart was aching, so I called my brother-in-law, who was my husband's brother and a great man of God. I knew he would give me godly advice on what to do. When I told him what had happened, it was not a surprise to him, he knew all about the other woman. His advice to me was, "Sister-in law, you have two choices. One, you can use the law of this land to try and resolve this issue, or two you can go to God and let Him work it out." Well, at that point in time, it was hard for me to make a wise decision because the pain I felt paralyzed my thoughts. I couldn't think straight. All I did was cry for a while. I was not ready to be a single mom with four children and driving cabs five hours a day with minimal money. I concluded I was in a real mess.

After thinking about the situation over and over again in my mind, bitterness and resentment set in. All I wanted was for my husband to experience the level of pain I had experienced, be it emotionally or physically. I had decided to be the one to inflict that pain. But, I thank God that I was still long enough for the Holy Spirit to remind me that vengeance is the Lord's and He shall repay. Even though in my heart I really didn't want my husband harmed, the scripture must be fulfilled. First, I began to examine my life to see if I had contributed to the failure of our marriage. I realized blaming my husband or myself wouldn't resolve anything at this point in our marriage. I decided to just forgive him, although he didn't ask me to forgive him. Maybe if he had been a little more remorseful I wouldn't have been so bitter. Then it hit me; I couldn't heal until I forgave him.

Through this very difficult experience I still wanted our marriage to work. I thought if I keep myself busy with the children and keeping the house clean (still working five hours a day driving for the cab), I felt that this nightmare would pass. Inside I longed for things to return back to the way they used to be during the happier times of our marriage. So, I decided not to bring up the situation again.

One thing I've learned in life is that when you choose to forgive someone (and you do have to) then you must let it go. Things went okay for a while, but I knew within myself that my love for him was dying. He didn't seem to care one way or another. I felt like if we were going to stay together then I had to be the one to make it work. However, God is the only one that can heal the heart of a man. He continued to spend most of his free time gambling and staying away from home. Many times he left his job and took his whole paycheck straight to the gambling house and would not leave until all of his money was gone. Many nights he gambled all night long and when he came home, he had nothing. He made me feel as though I was not supposed to ask him any questions. After staying out all night it began to affect his job performance at work. I was concerned about the company firing him and the possibility of him losing such a good job at Carrier Corporation. I began to talk with him about this situation. He told me that he was going to try to make a change because he realized that things had not been good for us for a while. Things did change for us long enough to give me hope. For a while, we started getting a babysitter and going out to dinner, just the two of us. I felt like it had been worth all the pain I had gone through. I realized anything worth having requires a sacrifice.

For about two years, things went well. By now I was pregnant again with our fifth child, a beautiful baby girl, Ronda. He managed to keep everything going while I was pregnant. I was convinced that he really wanted to be with his family until the day I gave birth to our fifth child. When I was in the hospital, my mother was staying with the other children. Every time I called home to speak with my husband he was never there. In fact my mother finally said, "We ain't seen him." The first thing rushed through my mind was "Oh boy, he is cheating again." When the day came for the baby and I to go home, he picked us up from the hospital, but he was so restless it seemed like he couldn't get us home fast enough. As soon as we got in the house, he said, "Okay, I will see you all later, I need to be with the guys." It was about 1:00 a.m. in the morning when he returned. He had been drinking so much he went straight to sleep. The next day he was up and off to work, and we didn't see him again until the following day. I knew then that I had been holding on when I should have been preparing to let go. This went on for about two years, and by now I was tired of it all. I was exhausted from spending so much time worrying about him and how all this was affecting the children. I knew things had gone full circle when I began to discover lipstick on his undershirt when I did the laundry. He was having an affair again for the second and final time.

I realized it was time to make a decision. I extended one last opportunity for him to let me know if he wanted this family and our marriage to work. His answer was a slap in the face; "Do whatever you want to do, because it makes no difference to me." It was at that point I knew our marriage was officially over.

The first thing I began thinking about was how would I provide for a family of six? Driving cabs for five hours was not going be enough and I knew it. I began to earnestly pray and seek God for direction asking Him what must I do. It was a very hard time for me then. I knew something had to be done, but I did not know how to do it. It seemed like the more I prayed the less God heard me. By now I knew that God was waiting on me to release everything to Him and stop trying to fix it myself. He wanted me to trust Him. You see I had been the one that was in control, hoping that if I did this or did that, things would be the way I wanted them to be in my marriage. I finally realized it takes two to make a marriage work. Since I was the only one willing to make it work, I felt I was fighting a losing battle. I asked myself, what must I do now? I realized at this point that I was about to become a victim of divorce, which I never wanted to see myself as. To me, divorce meant being alone, and it was hard visualizing raising five children by myself. Even after knowing that my husband had been in an adulterous affair, I was yet willing to forgive him and stay in the marriage. Some may wonder why I put up with this, but sometimes you will put up with a mess just to feel like you belong to someone. Once you get a revelation of who you are in Christ, you will see the difference.

CHAPTER FOUR

Living by Faith

I guess by now I was finally getting accustomed to the concept of taking everything to God in prayer. I think the reason it may have been difficult to understand at first is because I didn't have the luxury of having that kind of relationship with my natural father. There's something about a father and daughter, a bond and confidence that God grants. The scripture teaches that if our natural parents can give us good gifts, and we receive their chastening, should we not have a greater confidence and trust in God? We can't enter into the Kingdom of God unless we humble ourselves as little children. So, that's the reason I cleave to God as a little child, a young dreamer.

I believe God was trying to teach me that He knew the mind and heart of that young dreamer from Ellaville, Georgia who He was trying to comfort during her valley experiences and encouraged to dream and live by faith. No matter how old I had become I still needed to humble myself as a child and go to the Father. It's amazing how as children we're so eager to grow up and become adults, however, in most cases we still desire the affection of our parents.

It was time to begin to walk by faith. I needed a better job with better pay in order to sustain our family. I prayed to God for an answer. Sometimes He doesn't answer when we want, but He's always on time. A short time after my husband and I went through our dilemma, Miller Brewing Company opened a new plant in Fulton, New York about thirty miles from where I lived. When the plant first opened, I was not interested in working there because they made beer and at the time I personally believed that a Christian shouldn't be working in an environment like a brewery. But in Hosea 4:6, it says *"my children perish for a lack of knowledge,"* meaning I was about to miss the blessing that God had prepared for me because of religious tradition. Sometimes God will not allow even you to stand in the way when He is trying to bless you. My best girlfriend, Barbara Robinson, had been hired in one of the Miller plants. The second plant had called Barbara for an interview, so she asked if I would ride with her and I did. I had no intentions of getting a job nor interviewing, I was just a spectator. Little did I know God was making a way for me at that very moment, I was there sitting in the waiting room looking in a magazine, while God was using Barbara as the instrument.

After she completed her interview and was speaking with one of the personnel managers, he asked why did she want to work in the brewery when she had been hired in the canning plant which was one of their other new plants. She explained to him that someone from personnel called her for an interview (only later to find out that it was a set-up for me). She told him, "I have a friend here with me who is in the waiting room that also needs a job." He told her to have me complete an application. Still my religious tradition almost made me not want to do it, but I did it anyway. He mentioned that the company was paying very good money. I completed the application, and they called me in for an interview the very next week. I still was unsure if I was going to accept it, so after the interview a week later they called me to come back in for a physical exam. Meanwhile, I was going through the motion still not seeing God in this plan. Three days after the exam, they called me and said I had the job and asked when I could start work! By now I was tossed between two opinions. I knew I needed the job because it would help make things easier for taking care of the children. The other side of me was wondering what people would say. I began to pray, realizing that I had asked God to make a way. I knew it had to be God, because when the plant first opened, over five thousand people had put in applications and many were not hired. God had made provisions for me because I had no intentions of working for Miller Brewery. It was a set-up by God to have me at the right place at the right time. So, I told them I could start as soon as possible. My baby was two years old and I had a dependable older lady that was like a mother to me that could help me with the children.

The next week I started work. We were working twelve hours a day and it was very tiresome for me. We were working from 6:00 p.m. to 6:00 a.m. The good part about the twelve-hour shifts was that one week we only worked four days and had three days off to rest, and the next week we worked three days and had four days off. We had plenty of time to spend with our families. I thought my husband would be very proud of me for working and helping out with the bills, but it only made things worse. He started gambling so bad that he was losing his paycheck every week. Instead of my check helping him, I was the one that ended up having to pay all of the bills.

This went on for about four years and by now I was really fed up again! It really did not matter to me anymore if this marriage worked or not. I had had enough of this! When I confronted him again about the way things were going, he told me he should have never married me. He loved to be in the streets, he didn't want any responsibilities, and he had made a decision to leave me. He said I am leaving you and threatened not to pay any child support. By then it did not matter to me anymore. A few days later, he packed his car and drove to Florida. Before he left, he said don't try to get in touch with me unless it was an emergency (death). He said if it was an emergency to get in touch with his sister who was also in Florida, and she would know how to reach him. Twenty-one years had past and I have never had to call him for anything because I knew that I had a real relationship with Jesus Christ. I'll admit that is was not an easy transition. When he left me my natural side quickened and fear tried to grip me, but I had to prepare for what was yet to come. Everything that I had hoped for and dreamed of was now at its end. One part of me was relieved, but the other part still wanted to hold on to the dream (which was really more like a nightmare). In the midst of this storm, I knew that I was going to make it. I knew it was not time to give up, cave in, and quit. I knew that I was the only constant thing my children had in their lives. I had to be strong for them.

God gave me much favor with my in-laws. When I was going through troubling times, they were there for us. Sometimes, when families break up there tends to be a division between the two. I can thank God for my brother-in-law, John Simon, and his wife Bobbie Simon. He told me that he was going to be our "Ace in the hole" if we ever needed anything. He told me to call him before we called anyone else, and believe me, I had to call on him a few times. Every time I called them, they were right there. Knowing that they were standing with us was a great strength. It helped to know that we were not in the storm alone. When my children graduated from high school, they were there for them, offering their support. When my baby son graduated from high school and left for college, they made a decision to send him some money every month until he graduated from college. They have been with us during every event that has taken place after the divorce, and I am grateful.

CHAPTER FIVE

When You Don't Know What to Do

After experiencing many ups and downs in our marriage, divorce now seemed inevitable. Though I so desperately wanted my children to grow up in a home with both of their parents, I didn't have the strength to allow them to watch what appeared to be a living soap opera unfold before their eyes. The outcome of this drama wouldn't end with Hollywood fanfare, but probably tragedy. Oh how I dreaded even speaking the word from my lips. Divorce! Many nights I just cried, not necessarily for myself, but for my children and my husband. How does love grow apart? I think when we marry many of us don't spend adequate time establishing a spiritual foundation for our marriages. Instead, we focus on the natural attributes and features of the person. But as I learned, the older we become, accompanied with the many life challenges and storms you will face, it's the spiritual bond and connection that strengthens and enables you to weather the storm. I feel that was the determining factor in the separation between my husband and I. We grew apart because we had no or little spiritual relationship (bond/connection).

As a new Christian, I wrestled with the fact that divorce wasn't a part of God's plan for his people, however, what I didn't understand was that God doesn't force two individuals to love each other, it's a free choice. My husband and I had to choose to love each other and both commit to seeing our union whole and prosperous. I see it symbolically to the commitment we make to Jesus Christ. It requires both our commitment and love for even our relationship with God to work. The scripture declares, **"What therefore God hath joined together, let not man put asunder** (Matthew 19:6-8)." The key message is, what God has joined together. We must allow God to connect us spiritually and that can't happen unless we both are committed and connected to God. It was because of the hardness of men's hearts God permitted divorce. As a wife I felt defeated, as a mother I felt as though I had failed my children. There was one thing I was sure of I had to continue. I remembered reading in my Bible; "The race is not given to the swift nor to the strong, but to the one who endures unto the end."

However, when the day finally came when we watched my husband drive away, there was a look of despair in my children's eyes that caused my heart to ache. I tried with all of my being to be strong for the children, knowing that I was hurting just as much as they were. My oldest son said, "Daddy doesn't care anything about us." I tried comforting him by saying, "God will provide," but as many of you know sometimes we simply need the love and affection of another human being to ease our pain. For the next few days I prepared for assuming total responsibility for the affairs of our home (repairs, maintenance, etc.) and raising five children as a single mother. Fear tried to grip me while thinking of the storms ahead, but that small still voice inside assured me that God would never put more on me than I could bear.

Before my husband left he knew that our oldest son had been in trouble with the law, but it didn't matter to him at this point. My son became very rebellious about everything. He started getting in trouble in school and soon after that I found out that he had been introduced to drugs and older women. It seemed as though I was facing one storm after another, and the enemy was desperately seeking to take me down. Many times I had to fall on my knees and cry to God for help. He was there all the time and somehow I knew that He would never leave me or forsake me because my trust was in Him. One of the worst things that can happen in your life when you are in the midst of a trial is to allow fear to grip you. That is the first thing that will try to invade your mind. We have to remember that God said, *"Fear not for I am with you."* I can remember the times when my oldest son had to spend time in jail during this difficult period of his life. The devil tried to torment me with thoughts about the horrible things that could happen to him while he was in jail (fights, etc.). It was a real hard time for me. My husband had walked out and now my firstborn was facing a couple of years in jail. He was in and out of jail for a while and it was taking a toll on me. Through all of this, I was working twelve hours, coming home to clean and cook for my other four children. I was feeling guilty about what was really going on with my oldest son and constantly wondered if I had done something wrong that was the cause for all of this. I knew my son was dealing with rejection because he always wanted to be with his father, but his father never had time for him. I guess that explains the rebellious attitude he had toward life. If a father rejects his child and provokes him to anger, then who shall direct him to the Lord (Ephesians 6:4)? God has declared in Proverbs: *"Train up a child in the way he should go: and when he is old, he will not depart from it."*

I believe that God had gifted me with the ability to raise my child, however, there are some things that God intends for the father to contribute. It goes back to developing a spiritual foundation even in the life of your children, so they too can weather life's trials. All I knew to do was love him and be there for him as God was for me.

Just as I began to adjust with what was really going on in my life and the life of my children, along came another storm. I had worked all week long, and it was Friday night and I was glad to be getting some rest, I thought. My oldest son, now seventeen, was out of jail and had decided to move about seventy miles from Syracuse to Rochester, New York to try to make a change in his life. So that night after the children and I had gone to bed, the phone rang about 12:30 a.m. It was the operator telling me that I had an emergency phone call and I should call my aunt in Rochester right away. I knew then that something was wrong with my son. The first thing I thought was, "Is he back in jail again?" Well, it was worse than that. When I called my aunt, I asked her what was the matter with Jr. now. I was not prepared for what she had to say. First thing she said was, "Marjorie, don't get upset, but I have some bad news about Jr.; he's been in a fight, and one of his eyes has gotten busted out and they need you here right away." She said he was losing blood fast and that they couldn't wait for me to arrive before starting emergency procedures, they wanted me to get there as soon as possible. When I hung up the phone I was in shock. Here it was almost 1:00 a.m. and the other children were in bed asleep. We were in the midst of a snowstorm and snow was coming down like crazy. So I began to pace the floor and say, "Lord, take care of my child, you know I cannot leave here now." The Lord gave me peace and resolve about leaving the following morning so I could get the other children to the babysitter. Meanwhile, it continued to snow all night as both storms grew worse.

By morning my car was covered with snow. I called my girlfriend Barbara Robinson and I told her what happened to Jr. I asked her if she would ride with me to Rochester and she agreed. She came over as soon as she could to help me get the other children to the babysitter. Then we headed toward the thruway trying to get to Rochester in this bad snowstorm. We knew that the only way we would get there would be by the grace of God. The roads were so bad from the storm I could only drive 20-30 miles per hour. We were praying and asking God to take us safely to Rochester because we kept hearing on the radio that the thruway we were on was so bad, that they were talking about shutting it down and everybody was going to have to get off. But we kept on praying, asking God to take us through safely. We saw cars and trucks sliding off the thruway, but we kept creeping along, believing God would get us there safely. It took me three hours to get to Rochester (In normal weather it takes an hour). When we got there we thanked God for bringing us safely through the storm. Shortly after we got off the thruway we heard on the radio that they had closed it down. When we reached the hospital we found that they had already operated on my son; he had been in recovery and had been placed in his room. I was so overwhelmed to see him like that, but all I could do was thank God that his life had been spared. He said to me, "Mama, I didn't want them to call you, I didn't want you to see me like this." Well, you know that no matter how bad your child has been, when they need Mama, how can you say no? As I reflect back, I think mothers exemplify what the Holy Spirit is to the Church. God gave us the Holy Spirit to comfort, to help, and to teach us. I believe the Holy Spirit is the womb of God, Jesus Christ plants the seed, and the Spirit brings forth the newborn, as does the natural mother in the earth. What an awesome witness if mothers love their children and family from that perspective. I told him he was still my son, and would always be!

Sister Robinson and I began to talk and pray with him, hoping that this was going to bring about a change in his life. Since we couldn't leave to go back home that night because of the storm, we had to stay until the next day. The following morning we headed back to Syracuse to see about the children as well as get prepared for work Monday morning. I realized I had to place Jr. in the hands of God, because I had four other children that needed me as well.

Well, about four weeks had passed since the last incident with Jr. when I received another phone call from Rochester stating that he had been stabbed five times in his back and had been taken to the hospital. Here I go again, back to Rochester. This time I took all the children with me. By the time we arrived at the hospital in Rochester the administrators told me that they had drained and dressed the wounds and discharged my son from the hospital. I immediately went to the place he'd been staying thinking surely he went home and was resting, but to my surprise when I arrived his half sister told me that he had left with a gun looking for the five Puerto Ricans that had stabbed him earlier. We waited there franticly until night, still no word from him. I was praying for my son to come home safely. As I sat there thinking about my oldest son, I looked across the room at my other four children, realizing that I had to preserve myself for their future. I came to the conclusion that I had done what God had required from me as a mother. I had been a faithful steward over his child, realizing that if I had been faithful, God is much more faithful. I believed that this was a job for El Elyon, the most High God. Do you know that Jr. couldn't find the guys that stabbed him? I thank God for that, because there's no telling what would have happened if he would have found them while carrying that gun.

God gave me peace in the midst of the storm and I came to know that this peace is the Holy Spirit that lives within. This experience was more than I could bear, yet just another opportunity for God to be made strong. Remember in your weakness God is your strength and joy. We must know that God always has our back. The victory is in knowing that the battle is already won. We must know that nothing lasts forever, other than our life in Christ. No matter how the storm rages, the sun will shine and your good days will outlast your bad days. I thank God that now my oldest son Wardell is born-again and living for the Lord. He knows now that God is his only way out. So, mothers don't become weary in your well doing. When your child is out there, just pray for them and put them in God's hands, believing that God will make a change in their lives.

Thank God for change! You may be a victim, but you can become victorious. Never give up and always stay focused and God will vindicate your adversity. Although sometimes it may look like you are losing on every hand, be determined to win. The storms will pass and not last.

Chapter Six

A Cry for Help!

As time went on, things got a little better. Little did I know the storm winds were raging and another storm was coming. Thinking back to when I sat on the porch of my parents' home in Ellaville, Georgia dreaming of a wonderful life, I never saw myself divorced and having problems with my children. In a million years I wouldn't have pictured myself in this position. We never know what God has purposed for us and those whom we encounter in life. Maybe if I hadn't met my husband I wouldn't have met my sister-in-law Vera who asked me to attend that revival where I gave my life to the Lord. The Lord orders the footsteps of a righteous man and we should never forget that.

This next challenge involved my oldest daughter Laurie. I was heartbroken when I discovered at sixteen she was introduced to drugs. You can't imagine the devastation of seeing a child imprisoned by the lure and seduction of drugs. It's like they're not themselves and someone or something else has taken over their will. The signs became very clear when she started staying

41

away from home. Sometimes I wouldn't see her for weeks, even months. I didn't know where she was or if she was dead or alive. Countless nights I would lay awake wondering where my child was. Many nights I feared for her life, a young attractive girl on the violent streets of New York, anything was possible.

I got to the point where I was afraid to look at the news because every time I heard they found the body of a young woman, I would almost panic wondering if that would be the face of my daughter they found dead. You know the devil always wants us to think the worst until you take authority over him! It had been about two months since I had heard from Laurie and it was finally beginning to take a toll. All I could think about was my little girl whom I had loved dearly was alone and had gone astray. The anguish I felt as a mother not being able to help or be there for her during this difficult time. She was my first daughter and naturally I was very attached to her emotionally. She had been looking for love in all the wrong places. She was close to her father and now that he was gone, this was a desperate attempt to fill that void in her life. I knew she was involved heavily in drugs because people would tell me they would see her and try to make her go home. She would tell them that she didn't want me to see her like that. So she just stayed away, living on the streets and going from place to place.

One day I was watching the evening news and a bulletin came across the screen saying they had found a body of a woman around Laurie's age and that they would give the details later. My heart was pounding so hard that I began to pray, "Lord, please don't let this be my child." As I sat there with tears in my eyes waiting to hear who this woman was, to my shock, it was one of Laurie's friends; this child had stayed with me for about a week while her father was out of town. I was saddened to know that someone had taken her life and that her family would have to face such a tragedy. I knew she had some serious problems, but now her life was gone and the life of the baby she was carrying. As I prayed and cried, I realized that this was another job for El Elyon, because I really needed help in order to get through this storm before it destroyed me.

One night, about two weeks after the death of Laurie's friend, I was walking the floor unable to sleep, wondering where she was, even going to the window looking out to see if my child was coming home. I remembered crying out to the Lord saying, "Lord I need your help. I can't work staying awake all night long worrying about my child." I said, "Lord, You have to deliver me. I need Your peace." It was about 5:00 that morning as I lay in my bed meditating on the Lord, I heard, "Cast your cares on me for I care for you." Instantly calmness came over me and I fell off to sleep for about an hour before the alarm went off at 6:00 A.M. I got up and got dressed and went to work and worked all day. God delivered me that night and reassured me that the peace I sought was within, the Holy Spirit, the indwelling presence of His Son Jesus Christ. The reality of Laurie still missing was there, but He took the burden off of me. From that night on I was able to sleep every night, not yet knowing where my daughter was, but it taught me how to trust God. She went from bad to worse; she even spent time in jail and prison, but in the midst of those storms I had peace. It has been nineteen years, she's been through hell and high water, but until this day God has not allowed me to worry about her because I believe in due season she'll come to know the love of God our Father who is able to fill the void of her heart and save her to the uttermost

When you feel like all hope is gone and you can't carry on, just remember God will help you weather any storm. You're not alone! For He said, *"I will be with you until the end of earth."* He said He will not allow us to be tempted above that which we could not take, but will make a way to escape. I think it's important in Laurie's, and any other young woman's case, that we constantly preach the Love and forgiveness of God, even with the prodigal son in scripture, his father's love for him never diminished because of the bad life choices he made. He was willing to receive him with open arms when he returned home, not focusing on what he had done, but celebrating and praising God for keeping him. I praised God for being there for both Laurie and my entire family and for calming the abrasive winds of the storm. Most children forget or don't realize that parents were kids too and that they can find refuge with you. I always wanted Laurie and my other children to know they can always come to me.

Now that my two oldest children were out of the house, I was left with three more. My third child, Dolores, was not a problem child. She graduated from high school and started college; however, shortly after, she got pregnant and dropped out. We got through this experience as well. After having the baby Dolores decided to stay with me for a while until she was able to get back on her feet. By now my fourth child, who is my baby son Don, was getting ready for college. I remembered when he was getting ready to graduate from high school. The day before he graduated he was doing some last minute shopping when he became overheated and passed out on the streets of downtown Syracuse and ended up in the hospital. He suffered what the doctors called a grand mal seizure. Since he was a child he had these seizures when he became overheated. As a precaution Don decided to go to college in Atlanta, Georgia. I tried persuading him not to go that far away from home and to attend a college in Cincinnati, Ohio, which was closer to home, but it was his goal and determination to attend DeVry Institute of Technology in Atlanta.

After I couldn't get him to change his mind, we packed the car and took off for Atlanta. I did all of the driving, not realizing how much pressure I was under until I got back to New York. Some years ago I injured my back on the job and managed to keep going, although all the danger signs were evident in my body. I had to act like I was "Wonder Woman" in order to carry out all of the responsibilities I had to deal with. I felt like there was no way I could stop doing and being all to my family. In addition to my house, my car and all the other expenses that went along with this, I had just incurred another bill with my son going to college. His tuition expense was an additional $300 a month and I was not sure how I was going to mange it. Through all of the many disappointments one important lesson stuck with me, when I'm facing any problem I can cry out to God boldly, because He hears us and has mercy and grace in our time of need.

CHAPTER SEVEN

Can You Pass the Test?

After returning home from Atlanta, Georgia I could tell that something was wrong in my body, however, I assumed that it was due to the long drive and went along as usual with my daily routine. After going through so many mental and emotional experiences it drained both my body and mind. Yes, I spent a lot of time praying but I must have not left it all with God. I went to work one day having familiar thoughts about making ends meet at home as well as supporting Don in college, my budget and my pay checks were not adding up. It seems as though I was facing the impossible. Much of the stresses that I held in for so long finally began to manifest.

While at work one day I began experiencing severe pain in my lower back. Being the pillar of strength that I was I figured that if I could just make it to the car and drive the thirty miles home I would be all right. When I got home it felt like my leg was going numb. I managed to make it inside the house, but by then I knew something was seriously wrong. Through all the pain the only thing I could think of was my inability to follow the normal routine I had kept for years, such as going straight to the kitchen and starting dinner for the children. So I told my daughter I needed to go lay down, but as I started upstairs a very sharp pain hit me in my back and brought me to my knees. I stayed in the stairway a little while until my daughter was able to help me to my bedroom. Still, after all of this I thought that after a good night's rest I would be ready to go back to work the next day, but I was wrong again. The next morning I couldn't get out of bed by myself. I called for my daughter to help me get dressed. I was feeling very weak and knew that I needed help from God and a doctor.

Within a few minutes my daughter had the doctor on the telephone. She began to describe the symptoms I was experiencing, and without hesitation he told her to get me to his office as soon as possible. When we arrived at the doctor's office, he examined me and contacted a bone specialist and told my daughter to take me directly to see him. During this entire time I was assuming that the doctor would prescribe medication and send me back home to rest a few hours. I was sure that I would be able to return to work the next day. I didn't have time to be sick nor could I afford to miss time from work. After the bone specialist examined me and completed several X-rays, he said, "Get dressed and I will talk to you in my office." I was thinking, "What is he about to say?" As I sat down in his office, he began to explain that I had deteriorating disks in my back and that I should go get this prescription filled and go home and stay off my feet for a week. I was hoping I did not hear him correctly. I asked myself, "How could this be?" I had too much depending on me. I was thinking about my son, whom I had just enrolled in college, and all the other responsibilities that I had. I just could not allow anything to stop or slow me down at this time. However, I didn't stop to think that maybe God needed to spend some time with me. If he could slow me down physically maybe he could heal me spiritually and emotionally. I was thinking again, all I needed was a miracle or a quick healing, but God had other plans. The doctor didn't tell me how long I would be out of work; he just said to report back with him in a week.

I knew that a disability check would not be what I was making at that time. The most I could get for disability would be $300 a week, which was no comparison to the $590 I brought home weekly, and that alone barely made ends meet. So, I went home with all of this pressure on my mind, hoping the week would soon pass and that the doctor would release me to go back to work. Well, to my surprise, when I returned to see the doctor at the end of the week, he wanted to do more X-rays. Then he said to me, "I am going to give you a new prescription and I want you off your feet for a month." All I could think about was getting behind in my responsibilities and not being able to do anything about it. That's when I knew I had a serious problem, so I had to get serious with God concerning this calamity. I got before Him and I shared all the things I was facing, as though He didn't already know. Relief was nowhere in sight, it seemed, sounds familiar! All I could hear was "Cast all your cares on me and I will care for you." At the time I didn't know all the scriptures I could pull on to bring comfort, but I knew without a shadow of a doubt that God would not fail me now.

Each day I tried to make myself better by doing what the doctor said. Even though I took the medication for my back, it only put a band-aid on the pain momentarily and did nothing for my head. All I could think about was getting back to work after this month was over, because I had no savings account and was living from check to check.

49

A month passed and it was time to go back to the doctor's office. He examined me once again and said, "I want you out six more weeks." I looked at him and thought he was crazy. He really didn't know what was going on in my natural life. All I could think about was the possibility of the doctor extending my treatment to get money out of my insurance company. I was blaming the doctor, acting as though my back pain was his fault. In times like these we give the devil so much credit when sometimes God is working His plan. Did you know that all things must be ordained by God if He is the supreme authority, and we know that He is? So, nothing happens to us without Him knowing it before it happens.

Worrying about how I was going to get through this simply made things worse and frustrated me to no end. Notice I said I was trying to figure things out and not trusting God for the answers. I wanted to be in control of this situation, but God was in control of the situation. I had to realize that I had to completely trust in the Almighty God. How many tests would I have to endure before I truly learned to place everything in the hands of God and leave it there? As soon as I did doors began to open. As a young child, do we ever wonder if food would be on the table, or if we would have clothing to put on? No we trust that our parents would provide. So, why is it so difficult to trust God?

After allowing God to intervene a credit card company had sent my son a pre-approved credit card with a limit of $1200. Now you know that this was a blessing in disguise because I had no way of knowing how I was going to pay the expense of his tuition. He was able to charge that portion on the credit card until I was able to go back to work and pick up the payments again.

But wait, that's not all! God also blessed me through my church. My late pastor, Elder Seals, told me not to worry about my current situation. He said that I was a faithful member with my tithe and offerings, so during those three months that I was out of work, the church gave me over $1000. My son got a part-time job and he was able to bring in about $400 a month to help with his rent as well. He shared student housing with three other college students while in Atlanta until one of his roommates and he had a disagreement. Don called me and expressed his discomfort, so I began to pray on his behalf. God showed me favor with my sister Helen Stewart and her husband Jake who lived in Atlanta, Georgia. They offered to let my son stay with them. God blessed him to stay with them for ten months without having to pay for food or rent. That was a blessing and I am grateful to them for doing that. God met our needs according to His riches in glory, and not our limited expectations; I realized that I doubted Him because I was seeing things from my point of view. The scripture teaches that His ways are not our ways and are as distant as heaven is from earth. What God has done for me, He will also do the same for you. We must learn to praise Him and give thanks in all things, because He is sovereign and promises to meet all of our needs. Finally after three months, I was released from the doctor to return to work with certain restrictions. I was not allowed to push myself any more like I had in the past and God made that very clear. Of course I adjusted to that and was just thanking God for the strength to be able to return to work. After passing this test I made a decision to live one day at a time and be thankful.

CHAPTER EIGHT

Winning Back My Child!

How can I ever forget the experience with my youngest child Ronda? To see such a young mind oppressed and confused with such a hopeless outlook on life takes the breath from a parent who so desperately seeks to find an answer. At this juncture of my life I was so focused on getting back to work, that just maybe I forgot about how much my youngest child needed me. Not just a provider, but also someone to embrace her, to listen and to share her daily experiences with. Communication is normally the corporate in any failed relationship and it was no different between Ronda and I.

After returning back to work after three months things were slowly but surely getting back on track. But, as you can imagine, the devil is never on vacation and is always seeking an opportunity to put a kink in God's plan. I'm so glad that Christ has defeated him once and for all. He's merely trying to convince us that it hasn't happened. In my case he brought another test, this time with my youngest child Ronda. Haven't I gone through enough, I thought? Well, the devil answered me with a firm NO! He made it clear when my husband left that he wanted to destroy my children and me and was set on doing so. Who's report shall you believe? I decided to believe God's report that we're more than conquerors through Him that loved us and allowed Him to equip me for the challenge ahead.

My baby had begun to give me big problems. She was rebellious, bitter and angry and came against any authority, including me. She started skipping school and some days never returning home after school. It was so bad that when I left for work some days, she would go back to bed and not even make an attempt to go to school. The school was calling me wondering where she was and if I knew she was skipping school. The more I tried to discipline her the more rebellious she became. I soon realized she'd gotten involved with the wrong crowd and was headed in the wrong direction. Nothing I said seemed to reach her; it was as though I didn't exist in her mind.

After she followed her newfound friends around for a while I noticed it began to take a toll on Ronda physically and soon she became ill. She spent six weeks in the hospital battling depression and issues with her weight. As an attempt to help we sought outside counseling. Because of our strained relationship, there was very little I could say or do to get through to Ronda. After the family had gone through our first few counseling sessions, I found out that she blamed me for the breakup of my marriage. Her father left when she was only six years old so she never had an opportunity to develop a relationship with him. I never discussed their father around them because I felt that what went wrong was between the two of us and not the children. Besides, they were too young to understand what separation and divorce meant.

Maybe this was the right choice and maybe it wasn't. Ronda seemed to blame me for her father's absence. It seemed as though I was the cause of her loneliness and her not having a father in the house to develop a relationship with.

Though I was working many hours I visited Ronda at the hospital every night. I couldn't explain what I was feeling watching my daughter lie in the hospital, and to think I may have been the cause of it all. There were times when she didn't want me there and she let me know it by not saying a word during my visit. Although it hurt deeply, I continued to be there for her and continued to pray for her deliverance that God might loose the strongholds the devil had on her mind.

When Ronda approached the required six-week period for her release from the hospital, she was still depressed and resentful toward me. She told the staff at the hospital that she didn't want to go home with me, but to a place called "Freedom Village." She thought the word "Freedom" meant she could do as she pleased and not have to obey anyone, especially me. The problem was that in order to go to Freedom Village, the parent's income would have to be at a certain level to assist in covering program expenses for the child. At the time I was making over $40,000 a year, which met the income requirements, yet the facility required parental consent in order for Ronda to be accepted into the program. Seeing how unhappy and depressed she was, I was willing to do whatever it took to help turn her life around.

After the hospital made preliminary arrangements with Freedom Village, I was notified that transportation was not provided from the hospital and that I had to be responsible for getting her there. Being that Freedom Village was over two and a half hours away from Syracuse,

I asked my sister-in-law, Bobbie Simon, if she wouldn't mind riding with me. She agreed to go with me, knowing how difficult it would be to release Ronda into the custody of strangers. During our trip Ronda said very few words and I didn't know what to say to her without getting her upset.

When we arrived, Ronda and I were taken through the facility's orientation, which outlined all rules and regulations program participants had to comply with. Now the time came to discuss the cost and payment terms. Based on my salary, it would cost $425.00 a month for her to be there. Without reservation I paid the money and Bobbie and I headed back to Syracuse. As I was driving Bobbie back to her house, all I was thinking about was getting home so that I could cry out to God. I had so many questions in the back of my mind. What could I have done wrong that caused such damage? Why was Ronda so unhappy and why didn't she want to live with me? When Bobbie and I took her to Freedom Village on that Friday, that night all I could do was toss and turn, finally realizing the Holy Spirit was urging me to get up and pray for my baby girl's deliverance. I prayed for her total healing, believing that God would ease the pain she was experiencing at such a young age. Well, little did I know God was even working through Freedom Village to open Ronda's eyes and show her the realty of what she was dealing with. In one night, Ronda found out that the rules were too strict for her. She discovered there was no real "freedom" in the "village" after all. It was more like a prison to her because she was not accustomed to such rules, especially from a group of people she didn't know. This place was more for juvenile delinquents as rehabilitation before going to jail. Plain and simple, if you didn't obey the rules, you would be thrown out of the program.

Ronda realized her home was a palace compared to where she was. So she planned a scheme that would get her evicted from the program by rebelling against the rules. Ronda felt as though she was being held captive. The very next day she called and asked for me to come pick her up. I said, "What do you mean come and get you? You were adamant about living there, even your counselors stated that you wanted to be there. Besides that, I just paid $425.00 for your stay at Freedom Village." I wanted her to know at sixteen she had to obey somebody and that she couldn't have everything her way.

After much thought I decided that she had to stay since she chose to go there in the first place. Well, lo and behold they called me the very next day requesting that I pick Ronda up. I was sincerely hoping that she had learned a lesson from this experience, and to my surprise she had. Shortly after all of this, Ronda gave her life and her problems over to the Lord. She was born again and accepted Jesus Christ and the Baptism of the Holy Ghost. With this new outlook on life she got serious and made a quality decision to complete her studies so that she could graduate from high school. After high school, Ronda told me that she wanted to attend college, so I did what any loving mother would do, I acquired a loan to provide the necessary funds to get her into college.

After she left for college, she was the last one to leave home. I felt a big relief. Here I am 50 years old and for the first time in 30 years, I felt I was free at last. I had raised my children to the best of my ability so now it was time for me. I was alone and enjoying it and was learning how to love me. What happens sometimes in life is people don't take the time to love themselves. I was always busy making sure the children were well taken care of and making sure the house was clean and all the bills were paid. My life was on hold. To me it did not matter about how I felt about me. It only mattered to me that I had done my best for others. So now that all the children were gone, I thought it was my time. I knew I had a good job and didn't think I would ever get laid off. I was getting ready to enjoy life by doing some traveling and take some well-earned vacation so that I could live one day at a time. Well guess what, another storm arose in my life and this was a big one. The job that I had worked on for 18 years had decided to close their doors. Wow, this could have been devastating for me if I had not been anchored in the Lord.

My dreams for a little while were shattered as I began to wonder, "What was I going to do?" No job at 50 was very scary. Thank God my hope was not in the job, but in the Lord. I knew that He would make a way for me. In spite of all the negative thoughts that were coming at me, my faith kept me focused. All I could think of was, "What if I lose my home or what if I could not get another job with a disabled back?" How would I manage? I knew Ronda was in college and I wanted to see her graduate, but without a job I would not have the funds to help her expenses. After she found out I was losing my job, she decided to come out of college and get a job. I told her that I was not going to stay in New York anymore and that I was tired of the snowy winters that I had dealt with for 33 years. I had made a decision to move back home to Georgia where my son Don was living. He had finished college in Atlanta and had a good job and a two-bedroom apartment. He told me that we could stay with him, although he really didn't have enough room because my other daughter Dolores and my grandson JauQuin were already living with him. He was willing to make a sacrifice for his family because he knew that I was having

58

a hard time giving up my seven room home, but we made the situation work.

I was still having problems with my back, and so Don didn't want me to return to work. He knew that I was having a hard time so he decided to work two jobs to keep things going. I really had to pray for Don's strength, especially when he ended up one year working three jobs. He worked as a Sales Manager at a hotel, a part-time cashier at a grocery store, and as a data entry customer service representative 2-3 nights a week.

When Don was only 9 years old, he used to tell everyone that when he grew up he was going to get a good job so he could make enough money to make things easier for his mother. At such a young age he had my well being at heart. Little did he know there would come a time when he would have to prove himself. When I came to Atlanta to live with him and the rest of my family, he did everything he could to make life easy for me. He offered me his bed and said he would sleep on the floor, but I told him no. I said, "Son, you are the one working, so keep your bed and I will make me a bed on the floor." I was not too proud to do that either. Although it was a major test for me to leave my home in New York, to succumb to a floor in an apartment in Georgia, with the grace of God, I did it!

Galatians 6:9 says, *"Let us not be weary in well doing for in due season, we shall reap if we faint not."*

I thank God that in spite of all the trouble I went through with Ronda, God gave me the desire of my heart which was to see her born again and filled with the Holy Ghost. Well glory be to God, this has come to past. I encourage any of you that are currently reading this book to be patient and prayerful. In order for you to realize the same victory, God must be in control of your situation. Learn how to be thankful and allow Him to work on your behalf and in the lives of your children. God knows what's best for you and is concerned about everything that concerns you. He knows how as parents we love and care for our children and will not suffer them to see destruction. It takes waiting on God's timing and allowing Him to move when He gets ready to move. Our timing is not always God's timing. Although all of my children are not saved yet, I strongly believe that before they leave the face of this earth that they will be born again. Acts 2:39 talks about the promises for me and my children and so I stand on that promise for their salvation. Never let their problems or tests disappoint you. Do we have such a high priest who's not been touched with the feeling of our infirmities? The answer is No!

Psalm 37:4 says, *"Delight thyself in the Lord and He shall give thee the desires of my heart."*

So you hold on, due season always comes, my friend.

CHAPTER NINE

Speaking God's Word When You Are Going Through a Storm

Whenever I felt overwhelmed the Holy Spirit led me to write prayers that brought comfort during my valley experiences. I've included a few of them throughout this book as an aid for you as well. These prayers helped when I lost my job in New York and moved back to Georgia to live with my son. I knew God could and would restore my health and possessions. Even at my lowest point, I was confident that I would rise again. I believe God has the ability to do anything. He's just and righteous and will never forget our labor of love. He knew me in my mother's womb and ordered my footsteps. He never said there wouldn't be a storm, but He assured us that he would be with us and never forsake us.

God allows us to be tested because he's working each test for our good, confident that if we trust Him we'll pass each test with flying colors. Yes, we're eventually going to mount up on wings as eagles and excel above the traps and snares the enemy sets for us. I know sometimes it gets very bleak when you're trying to maintain your focus, but always think on the things that are good and are of a good report. The Word of God is truth and sanctifies us for the master's use. God has created us in His likeness and image and desires that we experience the fullness of his joy. He also desires that our light shine before the world, which is the word of God in us. God has a purpose for our lives and commands that we have joy even when faced with adversity, because the joy of the Lord is our strength. We have to be patient when problems confront us. We must stand firm and believe that we've already overcome the situation, and we're simply waiting for the manifestation. As you spend time with God daily, ask Him to renew in you a right spirit and restore the joy of your salvation. It's always good to return to the place of our conversion, rekindling your gratitude and appreciation for the ultimate sacrifice Christ offered at Calvary. While traveling life's journey it's important to remember that God's word is the lamp that lights your pathway, the reason that many of us become distracted and lose our way is because we refuse the instruction of God. How can we ever realize our destiny without God? All wisdom and knowledge comes from Him, He's the only one who truly knows the future. I pray that we all learn to wait on the Lord.

Go to God for yourself and stop running to everyone else all the time for the answers. When you're hurting, PRAY diligently before the Lord, the answer will be made known. Don't stop doing what you know to do. It's impossible to please the Lord without faith, and as you know faith only comes by hearing the word of God. Seek God daily and allow the Holy Spirit to abide and quicken in you His promises, which will preserve and keep you under the shadow of the Almighty and His might. Press your way into the presence of God, there you'll find strength, joy and gladness.

PRAYER

Lord I have a covenant with You and You have to make all grace abound toward me. You will bring it to past. Prosperity is mine...NOW and as a woman of covenant I make a quality decision to pass this test. Amen.

Always know that God can change those things in your life that aren't going right and those changes can happen suddenly. Your storm may last a day, it may last a week, or it may last years. Ask yourself this question; "What can separate you from the love of Christ, can death, persecution, pestilence, or spiritual wickedness? The answer is nothing! Your expectation that God will bring you through should be established by the fact that you have a High Priest being tempted Himself; he can secure those that are tempted. We must never waiver. Remember that our change is all the way.

Acts 1:4 states, *"If you want the promises of God, you must wait. After waiting, you shall receive the promises."*

There is a period of waiting that everyone must go through. God may have to work some things out of you during this "holding pattern" you may be in. Your part as a Christian is to believe that God can and God will do the miraculous in your situation. You must have patience and believe that He's given you the Anointing to remove and destroy every burden and yoke. I've seen people get fussy, impatient and busy about the wrong things, trying to force God to move on their time schedule and not during the appointed time of God. You can be busy doing the wrong things and guess what...get out of the will of God and miss your appointment for deliverance because of not waiting for His direction. You see, when you walk in fear

63

you block up the flow of the anointing and the blessings of the Lord. As stated earlier, perfect love (God's indwelling presence) casts out all fear! God wants to be able to flow freely and have complete control over your situation. Do you have God's hands tied? Are you allowing the Spirit of God to reign and control the lust of your flesh that's in constant conflict with the things of God? It's just like when a police officer puts the handcuffs on a criminal and puts the key in his pocket. What can the criminal do once his hands are locked behind his back? Absolutely nothing until the key is presented to unlock the handcuffs and his hands are set free. God wants to give you the key or the answer to your freedom from that bondage you are in, but you have to remain patient, seek him through prayer and fasting and wait until He drops the charges or completely dismisses the case that Satan has brought against you. The Word of God tells us in **Deuteronomy 31:8,** *"Fear not, neither be dismayed, for God is with us."* True victory only comes after the battle.

Jesus Christ is the key that unlocks the door to our freedom and inheritance. Faith is the bond that's been secured by the Death, Burial, and Resurrection of Jesus Christ. His blood is the payment for the transgressions of all mankind. Great is the Lord and Greatly to be Praised! The Lord will fight for us if we hold our peace, no matter what comes against you, as long as you do your part. Notice I said do your part and not get in the way of the things of God; He will deliver you out of all your turmoil.

Here is a prayer you can pray and meditate on while you wait on God.

PRAYER

Lord, my desire is to be used by You to do Your perfect will. I want to live each day and give My soul's desire is to be a vessel and to be filled by You. Hear my cry, oh Lord, and attend unto my prayer. From the depths of my heart I cry out unto You so that You may fill my cup. Lord, fill it up until it is overflowing. Lord, I want to be used by You to do Your perfect will. You, oh Lord, are a Shield for me. In You, oh Lord, I put my trust and You shall show me the path of life. In Your presence, I see the fullness of joy. You are my Rock and my Fortress. God, You are my Deliverer. God, You are my strength in which I put all my trust. Thank You Father, in Jesus' Name. Amen.

CHAPTER TEN

A Time of Bonding

After getting settled in Atlanta, I was able to go back and forth to Ellaville every weekend to see my parents. Ellaville is approximately 119 miles from Atlanta and about 10 miles outside of a town called Americus. I didn't realize how much I missed my parents until I was near them again. It did my heart good to be able to take my mom shopping, to lunch, or wherever she wanted to go. When I was with her I let her know that she was the priority and the focus of my attention. I was just glad to be back home, the place to which as a teen I so desperately wanted to flee. Spending time with the two of them again resolved many issues within me that I wasn't even aware existed.

I would usually spend at least three days with my parents when I visited with them. This fellowship went on for about a year before my parents' health started failing.

One day, my father had a bad accident while trying to load his tractor onto his truck. The tractor flipped over and pinned him underneath, but by the grace of God, his life was spared. He had to be taken to the hospital and ended up staying there for three days. I was in Atlanta when I got the news and without hesitation my children and I immediately left for the Americus Hospital to be with the rest of the family. Because of his age we were very concerned about him staying overnight in the hospital, so I stayed with him all night. After he was released from the hospital it took some time for him to recover. Meanwhile, I was traveling back and forth from Atlanta to Ellaville each week to offer what assistance I could. I was not able to do much because of my back injury, but God gave me strength to continue to make those trips just so that I could be there for them. Both of my parents were in their eighties and needed us to check on them periodically. Although they were able to take care of themselves, my father began to slow down from his normal busy routine. About two months later he became ill again. My oldest sister decided that it would be best to bring them both to Atlanta so it would be easier for us to take care of them. The same night we brought my parents to Atlanta we had to rush my father to the hospital to have emergency surgery to stop hemorrhaging from his brain. Following the surgery his condition seemed to worsen, however, we were still optimistic. After a short time in the hospital my father was dismissed and went to stay with my sister Helen until he was physically able to return to Ellaville. As I mentioned before there was something about the farm back home that my father was truly connected to. He requested that we take him back home, which meant taking frequent trips back and forth to Ellaville again. Well, about three weeks later my father suffered a major stroke that left him paralyzed on one side of his body. My father was never able to speak again after that tragedy. When the entire trauma began, he was in the hospital in Atlanta for a while. After the doctors did all they could do, it was time for the family to make a major decision concerning his health. He was totally dependent on someone to care for him around the clock, and that was something we just couldn't do. So, we made the decision to place him in a nursing home.

Shortly after all of this, my mother became ill. My father was terminally ill and, according to the doctors, my mother had brain cancer. They kept my mother in the hospital for what seemed to be an eternity, but later released her to stay at my sister's house. I would go over to the house and stay with mom every day. It was very hard to see the health of my parents failing so quickly. When my mother had to return to the hospital, she lived for about eleven more days. Three weeks later my father passed. For those who may have never experienced losing a parent, words cannot express the void. As a Christian we understand and have hope because of our eternal inheritance, but still the fact remains our natural refuge and safe haven is gone. We now must run to our spiritual Father who's always there for us.

It took some time to adjust to the reality that they both were gone. But through it all, with God's help the family and I made it. I share this testimony to encourage others who've had to face this same test. Just remember there is hope as long as you trust God, who is both the author and finisher of our faith.

CHAPTER ELEVEN

Surviving the Aftereffects of the Storm

Now that both Mom and Dad were gone it was as though I was starting all over again. Living in Atlanta, Georgia with my son Don was somewhat of an adjustment for me because I never had to depend on my children for anything, instead they were totally dependent upon me. I came to the conclusion that I was in Atlanta because of the will of God. I knew He had a greater plan for my life and me and preserved me from the destructive forces of evil. Many days it seemed as though I would lose my mind, but I hung in there, believing that this too shall pass. I realize that anything worth having requires a sacrifice, but many of us aren't willing to make that sacrifice. The Bible declares that where a man's treasures are, there shall his heart be also. For me it was God's Kingdom and my family; they were my precious jewels.

Even though I had come through the fire, God was still refining me as pure gold. As with most parents, I spent my entire adult life trying to shower my children with everything I thought they needed. I still did not understand that God was working behind the scenes enabling me to do it, as well as providing my needs. Nothing has proven to be too hard for God. I praise Him for all of His goodness. I praise Him for loving me enough to walk with me through such difficult times. Though I experienced some dark days, the sun shined again and God always assured me that He was concerned about me. If we're able to love our children and give them good gifts, is God not greater and filled with more compassion? God's desire is to share the riches of His kingdom with all that love him. I'm a living witness that He does!

God has shown me much favor because I've never been selfish with my life. During this transition period I must admit the situation wasn't the most ideal, however, I still tried to make the best of it. I've been misunderstood many times, but I kept on sowing good seeds. Now I'm truly reaping the harvest. So many people in life make such bold predictions about what they would never do, well I'm here to tell you if life throws you a curve ball you'll be forced to adjust or strike out. We're competing in the game of life to win, not just merely get by. Now at this late stage in my life it's time to begin preparation and training for round two. Not only must we exercise our physical bodies, but also our spiritual minds as well with the Word of God as our gymnasium.

Sometimes it may be hard to let go and allow God to have His way in your life. We're so accustomed to doing things in our own power that we never consider the supernatural power of God. He wants us to be free and happy, because He loves us more than we can ever imagine. Sometimes that's difficult to comprehend because we've not learned to love each other from that perspective. For instance, when you love someone you're willing to do whatever it takes to make him or her happy. You may say, Sister Marjorie, I don't have anyone special in my life to love, well guess what, you're not alone, neither do I. But, I have Christ and He is the Lover of my life. If you don't know Him, then I advise you to get to know Him. No one can love you like the Lord. *"Oh, taste and see that the Lord is good and his mercy endureth forever."* (Psalm 34:8). God is the same yesterday, today and forever more. His love is unconditional. Sometimes people will love you only when you give them everything they want, but God's love and grace are unmerited. A love that isn't based upon what you do, but what God has done through the life of His Son Jesus Christ. And in my most trying times God's love proved to be the only constant that I could depend on.

As I reflected on my current situation and living conditions with Don, God helped me to understand that I wasn't the first mother to have to sleep on the floor and I'm pretty sure I won't be the last. When things seem so dismal and impossible to bear, I always remember that somewhere in the world there's someone much worse off. God doesn't tempt His children with evil, yet He uses each opportunity to display His strength during our time of weakness. Some win; some lose; some choose to walk through; others choose to give up; some even commit suicide or fall into a state of depression. Yes, I faced the same choices, but something inside gave me strength to press through. Did I really make the right choice? Was it the fact that God chose me and was committed to my survival? Of course it requires our faith, but through His Spirit we might obtain our victory. I've learned that tomorrow isn't promised, so the best thing we can do is enjoy today. If you understand that storms don't last forever, then you'll realize the important thing is getting through them, even though from the outside it looked as though I was defeated. A single woman divorced, my physical body was failing and rebellious children. However, God would not allow me to accept what I saw in the natural, He opened my eyes to behold the beauty of His salvation and deliverance. David said; *"Be still and see the salvation of the Lord!"* It's true in those quiet times God speaks and moves on our behalf. The first fifty years of my life represent half of the course I must run, God's awaiting me at the finish line to award me with the crown of life. We must admit that we need Him and not wear ourselves out before the race really starts. We have a runner, Jesus Christ, who's gone before us and can instruct us on the best way to run the course based on our individual gifts. All we have to do is follow Him. Easier said than done. Persistence combined with perseverance provides the perfect ingredient for life in the winner's circle Jesus is waiting to carry you across the finish line and celebrate your victory. Press on; no one else in this world can take your place, God has chosen you.

I began to pray and encourage myself in the Spirit. I knew that being discouraged wasn't an option because I knew there was much more left for me to do. Not only in the life of my children, but in my life as well. My self image was lacking stability, even though I knew what God thought of me. Again, after all I'd been through I guess this was a natural response. Sometimes we seek the approval and acceptance of our peers because it makes us feel normal. I thank God that I was never the type to feel sorry for myself; I've always been a fighter. As usual the devil came to kill my vision of triumph, still my hope of glory, and destroy my confidence in God. But, I'd come too far to turn around. The most important thing was focusing my mind on the prize. Does it matter if I come in first or last? We all must finish the race!

Ecclesiastes 9:11 states, *"The race is not given to the swiftest nor the strongest, but to the one that endures to the end."*

Maintaining a positive attitude was essential to my survival. I never worried about what the Joneses had or what they thought of me because I knew it would draw me off my course. I never gave up, I never caved in, and I never quit. Stay steady and strong, don't become distracted with the affairs of this world, and keep your eyes and affections on things above. As with the Apostle Paul I'd become sensitive to the nature of God, if I only would look for him He would always show up regardless of the situation

II Corinthians 4:8,9 *"We are troubled on every side, yet not distressed; we are perplexed but not despaired; we are persecuted, but not forsaken; cast down but not destroyed."*

Understand that sometimes our problems help mold our future and no problem is without a solution. We must not put limits on our lives; we must trust God always and fix our hope on eternity. When we do that, nothing that happens in our brief lifetime can overcome or overtake us. In our suffering, we must remember that God is not our adversary; He's our Savior and Friend. We must expect to grow from our experiences. When we're absolutely trusting God with our whole heart, He rights every wrong that someone has done to us. So don't be easily persuaded to avenge your enemies; vengeance belongs to the Lord and Him only. In spite of our trials and tribulations we must work hard to prevent bitterness from taking over. What sacrifice is it to love those who love you? But loving your enemies requires sacrifice. **In Matthew 5:44, *Jesus told us to love our enemies and pray for those that persecute us*.** You may say, Sister Marjorie, "That may be easy for you to say." Well, my friends, I've been there. I've had to do what I'm proposing to you and it works. The choice is up to you. You can wallow in self-pity or you can walk by faith and know that you can do all things through Christ who strengthens you. Nothing can change until you make a choice to change things.

Think positive about your situation, talk to yourself and say, "Yes I can, and I will, overcome this." This trouble will not last always. Always strive to rise above that situation and know one day that it will be a thing of the past.

In Matthew 21:21, Jesus said, *"If you say to your mountain, be thou removed, it shall be removed."*

Understand that the greater the tests; the greater your victory will be. God's grace is sufficient! The greater the need, the more abundant grace He gives. If I had not learned and understood these principles, I would have given up a long time ago. But when I think about where I came from and where I am now, I have to say, "Glory be to God!" The only way we can fail is when we stop trying. A winner never quits and a quitter never wins! If our dependency is in God we should never fail because there is no failure in God. So why worry? Why be afraid? Why not trust your unknown future to an all-knowing God? He cares for you and me. We must be submitted and committed to His way of doing things, so stop trying to have your way all the time. Your prayer should be, "Lord, show me the path of righteousness and help me to walk therein." In the midst of temptations and trials, we must be patient and have endurance with longsuffering.

In James 1:2-4 the Bible says,
Consider it all joy my brethren when you encounter various trials knowing that the testing of your faith produces endurance and let endurance have its perfect results that you may be perfect lacking nothing.

Sometimes we're so quick to feel that we're the only one who's having problems and that no one really cares. We must know that whatever we do or whatever happens does matter to our Heavenly Father. He takes our victories and defeats very seriously. In Psalm 138:8 the psalmist says, *"He will perfect that concerneth us."*

Never let your past mistakes determine your future. In Philippians 3:13-14 *"Forgetting those things that are behind and reaching toward what is ahead, I press toward the goal to win."* We must be bold and courageous, always keeping an open mind in any situation. Don't just say, "This is me and that is the way it is going to be." Be willing to listen to sound counseling and if there are things that need to be changed, just know that you can change them. Some people will never receive victory because they are too quick to give up. Look at your results, because I heard a preacher say once, "A person that keeps doing the same thing the same way and expects to get a different result is defined as insane!" If you desire to overcome an addiction, wouldn't it make sense to speak to someone who's already accomplished it? Life is based on principles. Get the formula and just do it!

God is not a respecter of persons, but He is a respecter of Faith (Acts 10:34). If God has permitted His principles to work in the lives of others, He'll do the same for you. Our problem is that we're too quick to criticize another person. Just simply have the faith the size of a mustard seed and all things can become reality. Mark 9:23 states, *"All things are possible to them that believe."* The sky is the limit; you CAN have what you say according to the will of God! Matthew 9:29 states, *"According to your Faith be it unto you!"* For me, I've decided to trust God and believe he'll do just what he said.

TESTIMONY:

I can remember when I was going through a very dark time in my life. My house in New York had gotten behind in mortgage payments, and the bank was calling and writing me letters threatening to foreclose on my home. My mother was dying the doctors had given her up. My father was also at the point of death; I was going back and forth to see him during the day at the nursing home and staying nights at the hospital with my mother. I remember coming home to my son's apartment one morning; my heart was very heavy due to all the things that were coming at me. I just fell on my face and cried to God, "I don't understand all of this, but I know You have a plan." He comforted me by saying, "Trust in Me." Later that day my son came home and asked me, "Momma, what are you going to do about our home in New York?" He knew that I was about to lose the home, so I said to him, "What can I do?" At that point I wasn't able to work and had no way to pay up the note. It was almost $1000 behind and he didn't have any money either. But little did I know, God had a ram in the bush. Just like Abraham when God asked him to offer up his son (Genesis 22:13), God wanted to see Abraham's faith and I believe He wanted to see where my faith was as well. So I told my son, "It's in God's hands," but he didn't quite understand what I meant, that God was our only provision for saving the house. Being young with little experience with God he told his sisters, "Mama is going to lose our house."

It hurt him to just stand by and see twenty-five years of struggling to pay for this house and possibly lose it all to the banks. It was about three days before Christmas and we weren't planning to have a "Merry" Christmas that year, because we were losing too much that had meant so much to us. We were losing my mother, my father and my home. My daughter Ronda shared with her fiancée what was happening to my house and by him being a man of God, he began to pray for me that God would make a way for me to get the money. He said that as he was praying, God spoke to him and said, "You give it to her". So, they planned a dinner for me at his apartment to try to cheer me up and when I got there, they told me they were going to give me my Christmas present early. They presented me with a Christmas card with the amount of money I needed to save my house. I was so excited! Little did I know that this was the new beginning God purposed for me. I went to the hospital that same night to stay with my mother, feeling as though a weight was lifted from my shoulders. The following morning I called the mortgage company to inform them that I had the money. With excitement I said, "This is Marjorie Simon, the one you've been threatening to begin foreclosure procedures on my house in New York. I have the money, so can you please stop the foreclosure." The lady said "Ms. Simon, it's funny that you called, I have your papers in my hand right now and was in the process of proceeding with the foreclosure." She said, "You must wire the money to me today in order to stop the process." Thanks be unto God! I was able to wire the money and save my home. God may not move when you think He should, but He's always on time. I can remember the anxiety and desperation I almost yielded to, but in the midst of it all I had resolved that God's will be done no matter what.

The Scripture teaches that God has clothed the lilies of the field and feeds the birds of the air, and he's as concerned about us and our needs. All we have to do is seek first the Kingdom of God and His righteousness and all these things shall be added to us. My friend, God is patiently waiting with His arms wide open to receive you and pour you out a blessing that you won't have room enough to receive. Then you can say as I did, "I am a survivor."

PRAYER

Father I thank You for wisdom, revelation, knowledge, and understanding. I thank You for leading and guiding me in the path of righteousness. Thank You that nobody but You sits on the throne of my life. Because You sit there I have love, joy, peace in the Holy Ghost. Thank You for being my Shepherd and now I want for nothing. In Jesus' name I pray. Amen.

CHAPTER TWELVE

Weathering the Storms

Father, I thank You in the Name of Jesus for giving me the victory through these storms. In Jesus' Name, Amen.

God has also taught me through experience that love is able to bear all things, endure all things, believe all things, and that love never fails. I'm able to weather the storms because of this eternal hope and power dwelling within, the power of Love. When you're hurting and going through a test, you must be honest with yourself and admit that you're indeed hurting. So many people try to fool themselves into believing that everything is all right and that they can handle the problem alone without any help from God. However, as many before us have found out, without God we can do nothing, but with Him all things are possible. We must first acknowledge that the pain exists, and then take it to God in prayer. Yes! The one who is able to do exceedingly and abundantly above all we can ask or think of Him. If we never confess our faults, how can we expect God to heal us? I believe many have hindered the Holy Spirit from moving on their behalf simply because they were too proud to seek God for wisdom and knowledge. If we would only walk in God's wisdom then we would realize the prosperity and wholeness God promises every believer. God declared that if any man lacks wisdom let him ask of the Lord who gives liberally to all.

As I think back over my divorce and the effects it had on my children and me, I never stopped to think that the fallout could cause emotional damage and lead to some of the physical manifestations which I witnessed in the lives of my children. Emotional bondage only leads to a life of fear, loneliness and self-pity. I'm sure you've attended a few pity parties of your own. After awhile, you get tired of seeing your name as the only name on the guest list, day after day. How do we begin to unlock the prisons of our mind? I feel that the answer is by us yielding total control to God, surrendering not only the problem but also our will. Never let your problems control you, they're merely opportunities for God. You must take control of every situation in your life and realize that God "has your back." The way that you take control is by getting out of the way and allowing God to have control. It's been said that emotional pain can be more traumatic than physical pain. God constructed the body with the ability to heal itself with proper counsel. However, the Spirit heals the inner pain of the mind. If you continue to ignore emotional pain it will only dig deeper and sprout roots to the very core of your insides and eventually bring forth fruit after its kind. You'll end up resembling the double-minded man described in scripture, one who's tossed from one side to the other, having no foundation. And for a while that's what our life seemed like, storm after storm with no sign of the end being near. I thank God for having control of our life reins.

I'm sure you've had your husband or mate get on your nerves or the children or even your friends. You start picking out things about them that you don't like, but fail to do anything about. I think it's important for you to do as I did, first remember that they are God's children and are precious in His site. No matter how horrific the offense we must always be ready to forgive. The act of forgiveness requires love, which is the greatest attribute of the Spirit. Sometimes we put unnecessary pressure on ourselves due to circumstances and situations beyond our control. We must learn to let tomorrow take care of itself and enjoy today. The most effective tool to destroy the strongholds of emotional bondage is love. **1 John Chapter 4 states that** *whosoever loves is born of God and knows God because God is Love*. And that perfect love casts out all fear and worries that torment us. After all we had been through as a family the enemy's attempt to rob us of this precious gift called love was futile. The trials were merely developing patience, and through patience hope (faith). Love is the life source of our faith and without it faith cannot work (Galatians 5:6). Many times we're irritated with others because love is waxing cold due to life's pressures. Regardless, we must cherish each day and care for those we encounter, never knowing who we're entertaining.

I can remember when I heard those words from the mouth of the woman that was sleeping with my husband. She was very blunt when she called and said, "This is the woman your husband has been sleeping with." It was as if someone had taken a knife and performed open-heart surgery on me without any drugs to numb the pain. Now, had I not been anchored in the Lord, this would have thrown me for a loop. How can anyone in their natural strength endure such heartache? If it hadn't been for the abundant love of God (El Shaddai), that experience could have destroyed me. It was more than I could handle and it took love to constrain me and keep me in God's will. Needless to say, I watched God walk me right through that whole situation. If I hadn't gone through times of tests and trials I wouldn't have been able to write this book so that God could help others who may have to face the same trials. I believe that these testimonies not only gave me the victory after each storm, but also would allow others to see that they too can be victorious. They will allow others to see that they too can have peace and total victory over any negative situation that arises.

You may not understand why things in life happen the way they do. Some say it's our experiences that make us strong. Take it from me, you can make it through, I've been there. I'm not talking about Shadrach, Meshach and Abendego in the Bible. I'm talking about me, Marjorie Simon, real and in living color. We have to know that life is full of trials and triumphs. As long as you live you'll always be tested. The devil doesn't want to see you happy; his sole purpose is to kill, steal and destroy (John 10:10). Don't be ignorant or become dumb and think that you are exempt from tests and trials. Sure, you are going to have to face the test, but you must be confident that your outcome has already been determined because of your faith.

For whatsoever is born of God overcometh the world: and this is the victory that overcometh the world, even our faith. Who is he that overcometh the world, but he that believeth that Jesus is the Son of God?
(1 John 5:4-5)

Believe that you've overcome! I've always said, "Come hell or high water, I'll make it." Once you've accepted in your mind you're victorious you can experience the freedom Christ brings. Whom the Son has set free is free indeed! Lay aside the old and put on the new, from victim to victorious. You must walk in love because that is the birthmark of all believers. Never become weary; continue to press through to your destiny. You may have heard the story about the man who was complaining about not having any shoes on his feet. Well, once he saw a man who had no feet to put shoes on not complaining, he stopped complaining and began to be thankful for what he did have.

When you feel that your problems are so bad that you cannot take it, just stop for a few minutes and realize that there is someone else worse off than you. In Psalm 126:5, the psalmist reminds us that although we sow in tears, we shall reap in joy. Learn to endure whatever you need to endure, but this time, do it knowing that your joy is on the other side.

One of the major reasons God came to earth was to redeem man. To reconcile (restore, rejoin) man to Him. God's desire was to restore man's relationship with Him, that man could find grace, mercy, joy and strength in His presence. How was God able to draw sinful man and cause him to repent? Romans 2 states that it is the goodness of God that leads men to repentance. How amazing it is that God is able to forgive and forget man's transgressions? Simple. His love for man supersedes his (man's) deserved judgment. If we are to love one another as God has loved us, we should receive the same results. Now I understand why God allowed me to still reach out to Ronda when it seemed as though she wanted no part of me. By continuing to love her, love was able to draw her in and mend the brokenness of both our hearts. Only then could our relationship be restored.

Isaiah 25:4 talks about how God is a refuge from the storm. When you believe God for your deliverance, you must stand no matter how rough things may get. You have to allow yourself to be rooted and grounded in the things of Christ with your mind made up. My attitude and my heart are fixed. On Christ the solid rock I stand, when all others are falling like grains of sand, yet I stand!

TESTIMONY:

I can remember when I drove sixty miles a day traveling back and forth to work for eighteen years. It didn't matter if there was a bad snowstorm, rainstorm or personal storm in my life; I had to go to work. Sometimes the weather would be so bad the schools closed and the roads shut down so that we were unable to go to work. One morning, after working twelve hours the night before, I left work trying to get home to my children. The temperature was sixteen degrees below zero. It was so cold that all I wanted to do was get home out of the bad weather and get some heat and some much needed sleep. As I started down the highway, I noticed that my car began to run hot. I started praying, "Lord, help me make it home out of this bad weather." I kept on driving for about another five minutes, but then smoke was everywhere. All I could do was pull over off the highway and try to find help. Later, I found out that the head gaskets were blown.

While I was stranded out there on that highway, every car and truck that I tried to wave down went right past me as if I didn't exist. My hands and feet were beginning to get numb, so I got back into the car. By this time, the inside of the car was just as cold as the outside. I began to pray again, "Lord what am I going to do? I am trusting and depending on You to come to my rescue." Well, a small voice came to me and said, "Stand back outside." After another ten minutes of trying to wave down a vehicle, I still was unable to get someone to come to my aid. As I attempted to return to my car, a gentleman pulled up behind me and wanted to know how long I had been waiting outside. I told him about fifteen minutes. He stated that he was on his way to work, but very concerned that I'd been outside in this freezing weather for so long. He asked me where I lived; I said about twenty-five miles away in Syracuse, NY. Do you not know that this man was nice enough to take me all the way to my house and wouldn't let me pay him for being a blessing to me? Don't tell me that God won't provide for you. I'm a living witness that no matter what kind of storm you are in, there is a breakthrough for you.

Six Steps To Weather Any Storm:

Step #1: Remaining Steadfast

Your soul must be <u>anchored</u> (<u>steadfast</u>, <u>unmovable</u>) in Jesus Christ and you must be confident that God is on your side. You have to know that you can and that you will make it no matter how the winds may come and go. You must learn how to obtain peace even in the midst of a storm. My son reminded me how amazed he was when he knew I was going through a turbulent situation and yet always had a song in my mouth and victory in my heart. It helped me when I began to sing songs of praise to the most high God. In the presence of the Lord seemed to be where I obtained my peace. Yes, it's going to be rough! The key is, you have to see your victory before you can receive the victory. Tapping into the things you need to manifest in the physical realm must first be touched in the spiritual realm. Remember when Paul and Silas were beaten, chained down and thrown into prison? *"But they sang a song until God set them free from the prison."* (Acts 16: 23-26).

Step #2: When You Are Being Tested

Being <u>cheerful</u> can make your tests easy. God admonishes us to be thankful in all thanks and we can know that our faith in Christ has gotten the victory. Seek God for understanding when there is none to be found. Seek God for joy when joy can't be found. I declare if you seek God, whatever you need shall manifest itself completely in your life. He said that He would not put more on you than you could bear. God knows that the battle is already won. He knows just how long it will take for you to endure that trial and get results. The storm will pass. Nothing lasts forever, whether it is good or bad. Always know that it's possible for God to change things "suddenly," when your expectations are set high and your faith is sealed in knowing that He will.

Step #3: Maintain Focus

Sometimes you may have to wait a while, but you must believe that the victory is yours each time you go into battle. You cannot expect victory if you allow fear to grip your struggle. Picture yourself in a tug-of-war with God. Do you hear yourself saying, "Lord I need your help, but I can't commit to what you want me to do?" He's pulling you one way and you're steadily trying to go another way. You must know that God will never let you go because He's your protector and He loves you too much. God is your shield and your strength. Think on that and allow it to encourage you. Feelings of loneliness will flee when you realize where your help comes from. You may find yourself crying out to God in desperation for a companion or friend. He's attentive to your cry and sees your tears.

He'll be your strength and He'll shield you from all the fiery dots of the enemy if you allow Him. *"If God be for you, who can be against you?"* (Romans 8:31).

Step #4: Be Patient, Help Is On The Way

When God is for you, there is no need for you to be upset with yourself or anyone else for that matter. God "has your back" even when you're being mistreated. You're in a covenant with God, meaning we're in a relationship with God and He's promised never to leave you nor forsake you. He now sees you through the life of Christ, the Anointed One; holy, blameless in love. You must completely depend on God in your times of storms.

Take God off of your lay-away plan. So many times as Christians we act as if we can't take God for what His Word says He is. We put Him on lay-away and go back and forth to church making payments to hopefully one day see the manifestations of His glory. When things don't move on your behalf as quickly as you'd like them to, you find yourself getting upset at God because He's not moving according to your timing. The first thing you need to do is check yourself. Make sure you are in right standing with the Lord before you can place a demand on a storm-free life. Is your attitude right? Are you being dedicated to sowing into the kingdom of God with your finances? Are you totally allowing God to order your steps? If not, then the storms that come into your life are granted the opportunity to rain, sleet, or snow all over your complacency or your ill will to change.

Step #5: Humble Yourself

Be ready to make a change! Philippians 3:14 says, *"I press toward the goal for the prize of the upward call of God in Christ Jesus."* Sometimes we block our blessings by not having a willing heart and a motive for change. If getting through your storm calls for a press, then press on. God will instruct you when, where and how to move in such a strategic way that your struggle becomes an effortless one. God provides grace to match every trial and meet every challenge. You just have to remain encouraged and know that God has your enemy's final outcome in the palm of His hand. One reason we become discouraged is because we're impatient while God is establishing his plan to move on your behalf. Proverbs 16:7 says, *"When a man's ways are pleasing to the Lord, He makes even his enemies live at peace with him."*

Step #6: Forgive

Forgiveness plays an important role in your transition from one place to the next. If you are still walking around blaming yourself or blaming others for things that happened months or even years ago, then you aren't ready to go where God wants you to be. Remember, Philippians 3:14, *"Leaving those things behind, I press toward the goal."* It's virtually impossible for a runner to obtain the gold medal if the runner is weighed down with baggage. A small thing such as not forgiving yourself, or someone else for that matter, can keep you not only in the storm, but also in last place in a lot of areas in your life. Mark 11:25-26 says, *"Whenever you stand praying, if you have anything against anyone, forgive him or her."*

Pertaining to my experience, I had to forgive my father. I felt that I wasn't treated fairly by him concerning the distribution of his estate. When my father was alive he had over 200 acres of land down in South Georgia. I found that he had only left me 9.1 acres and divided the rest between my two sisters. Although I was very hurt, I had to make a quality decision to forgive him right away and move on. I now know that if I hadn't walked in love, God couldn't have blessed me the way that He did. I thank God that I know that I am bought with a price. Paid in full with the precious blood of Jesus Christ. My life is not my own and I choose God's perfect will over everything that I say and do. I thank God that I am free and I am living a glorious life and know that God is on my side. I thank God that the victory is more precious than all the suffering that I had to go through. As I continue to follow Christ, He shows me so many awesome things that continue to blow my mind. I thank God for all the tests and trials because I have the blessings of the Lord upon me. I found that once He blessed me like He has, it was hard to keep it to myself. My natural and spiritual children reaped from the blessings. Those that were there with me through the storms reaped the blessings as well. See, we are not blessed just to benefit ourselves. We are to share the blessings so that the windows of Heaven can continue to be open over our lives. Try not to get new and distant when the storm passes. Stay humble and remember this will help bring your deliverance that holds the keys to your success and prosperity. No matter what storms you may have to weather, just know they will pass and not last.

PRAYER:

Father, I thank You in the Name of Jesus for giving me the victory through all of these storms. Amen

CHAPTER THIRTEEN

Left Alone, but Not Lonely...

*When you've been through a divorce or a loved one
has left you.*

Have you ever been left alone, but never felt lonely?
Think about it, "Left alone, but not lonely". Is it possible
to be alone and not lonely? These two words could be
depressing if you didn't understand their true meaning.
Some people can't stand the words, "alone" and "lonely."
They're quick to think the worst about themselves and are
deceived into thinking that no one cares for them. You
must be strong, learning to walk by faith and not by sight
regardless of what you see before you. The will of God for
your life is for you to stand before Him holy, blameless, in
love, which He declared before the foundation of the world
(Ephesians 1:4). If He's purposed, who can change it? No
one!

THINGS THAT WILL KEEP YOU GOING:

Don't ever become anxious for nothing. First, seek
out the plan that God has already established for your

life. Being single is one of the greatest gifts you can have because you have more time to share yourself with the Lord. You need to continue to develop your character according to God's Word. Gird yourself up in the power of his might and walk therein. You can develop your character by being trustworthy, loyal, and creating a good self-image. Be the person that you want to be and the person that God wants you to be. You don't have to believe nor accept that you're in a state of loneliness. Do things that are beneficial to you and others and don't become selfish with people or things just because you're single. Don't find yourself concerned about what someone else is doing either. It doesn't mean that you're supposed to do the same thing he or she is doing. Just because someone else is committing adultery it doesn't mean you have to. Just because someone else is "looking for love in all the wrong places," it doesn't mean that you have to put out a search party of your own for Mr. or Mrs. Right. Be diligent in the things of God. Know that you'll never have to feel like you're less of a person or not whole because you're single. That's a trick of the enemy and you need to open your eyes and see his works. The enemy knows that if he can get you to feel lonely and depressed, then he can enslave both your mind and body. Some people spend their entire lives seeking material wealth and companionship. But godliness with contentment is great gain. According to Colossians 2:10, you are complete in Him, which is the head of all principalities and powers. You can grow in grace and in the knowledge of our Lord and Savior Jesus Christ. Flow in His wisdom and learn how to be content with where you; are; keeping the Lord God first. One benefit is to be able to study God's Word. By getting quiet and meditating on His Word, He can perform His perfect work in you. Don't bother God with silly questions like, "When God? When am I going to find my perfect mate?" or "Why God? Why am I not married yet?" There have been many times that I could have asked those same questions to God. I had to realize that God had a purpose for my life and it was only going to be revealed in His own timing.

He says in I Corinthians 10:13,

There hath no temptation taken you, but such as common to man. God is faithful and will not suffer you to be tempted above that you're able, but will make a way for your escape so you can be able to bear it.

After being married for seventeen years and ending up in a divorce, I had ample reason to feel lonely, depressed and even desperate. Some women feel like they're not whole when they go through a divorce. A divorce can allow you to feel empty if you allow it to. Take it from me, my sisters, when you have Christ in your life, you're never alone. He says in Hebrews 13:5, *"Be content with such things as you have."* In Deuteronomy 31:6, He encourages us to be strong and of good courage.

We're not to fear nor be afraid, for the Lord our God is with us. He'll never fail us. I can count numerous occasions in my life when I was tempted to throw in the towel. It didn't take long for me to remember that we're a peculiar people, a royal priesthood. I'm a child of the King, the most-high God. I had to remind myself that if God is for me, then who can be against me (Romans 8:31)? He said in Romans 8:37 that we are more than conquerors. I came to the realization that God loves me so much; He's the reason for my success and my children's success. Guess what, He's the reason for every good thing that comes to me. Ask yourself this question: What can I render to the Lord for all of His goodness? We must learn to be thankful and praise God more for the things He has already done. He is the reason for your success! Isn't He worthy of the praise for what and who He is to you? No matter what's going on in your life, God deserves the praise. Praise brings you into the presence of the Lord. It tells Him how much you love Him and how much you appreciate His love for you. You know how you feel when someone praises you for a good deed you've done? Well, God deserves the glory for the mighty works of His hand. He's a jealous God and would have no other God before him. Do we only pray to God when we need something from Him? You don't like how it feels when someone uses you, so imagine how God feels. The bottom line is in all things give God His deserved praise. You see, that's the difference between God and man. You wouldn't bless someone that did you wrong or showed ill will toward you now would you? However, that's the nature of the God we serve, loving those who despitefully use us. Ephesians 5:20 states, *"In all things give thanks."* That means the good, the bad and the ugly.

You can miss your blessing by not acknowledging the Lord. When things arise that aren't comfortable, you've got to learn how to trust in Him with your whole heart and lean not to your own understanding. Acknowledge the Lord in all your ways and He'll direct your path and lead you into all righteousness. In everything acknowledge His presence, His tender new mercies and His compassion. Don't be too proud to go to the Lord as a child would go to his/her parent when they are in need. God is waiting on you to acknowledge His authority and sovereignty with godly reverence. The fear (reverence) of the Lord is the beginning of knowledge. So let him operate on your behalf. He's in the fire with you and will get you through the rough times. When my children were small all they knew was "Mama" this and "Mama" that. They knew that if they fell down and hurt themselves, the first name to call on was Mama. If Mama did nothing but kiss their bruise and said it will be all right, then they were okay, because they trusted that Mama could soothe the pain. That's the way God wants us to be with Him. He's given us His Word and that should be enough. He said that Heaven and Earth shall pass away before one of His promises or Word fail us.

You must pursue God more than your dream mate. You know how you can be when you are in love, your heart aches after that man or woman. All you have to do is just hear the mention of their name and your heart and adrenaline starts increasing in speed. That's what the Name of Jesus does for me. There is no greater name on Earth than the name of Jesus Christ. See, my Bible tells me that every knee shall bow and every tongue will confess at the name of Jesus. (Romans 14:11) By no other name in heaven or in earth are we required to be saved by other than Jesus. There is so much power in His Name. There's Healing power, saving power and delivering power in His name. When your heart is breaking, there is peace and joy in His Name. When my husband walked out on me and left me with five children to raise alone, he left me there with no support whatsoever. I sincerely thank God because He (God) continued to be my source. He has been and is my strength. He is my friend and will be whatever you let him be. Many times I have had to throw myself on the mercies of God. Crying out to Him for help and waiting His appointed time was not easy. I can remember days and nights I shed many tears. The saints prayed with me and encouraged me to hold on and reminded me that trouble doesn't last always. My former pastor's wife, Sister Bessie Seals, would always quote the scripture in Galatians 6:9 which says, ***"Be not weary in well doing, for in due season you will reap if you*** *faint not."* That scripture kept me going. Sometimes people wondered why things aren't happening for them. You must check your life to see if your faith is wavering in your well doing. Have you missed your due season? If so, it's not too late to repent and get it right.

What will be your attitude when it's time to reap the harvest? Will you be grateful for the leftovers or will you be expecting the abundance God grants to the righteous? Life has been very unkind to me, but I am free now. My ex-husband can tell you that I never treated him wrong. For all he left for me to handle, I could have been a very bitter woman. But because I know that vengeance belongs to God and that He would repay, I released it and put it in God's hands and that settles it. God is concerned about everything that concerns you. All you have to do is make sure you are in right standing with God and He'll do the rest. I worked at my job for eighteen years. A job God gave me when I was in need of a good place of employment. He gave me the job four years before my ex left. God knew, as He always does, what was best for me. He knew that I would have to take care of my five children and take care of a home and a car as well. He blessed me with a good job so that I was able to take care of the expenses that came my way.

I could say like David said in Psalm 37:25,

I have been young and now I am old, yet have I not seen the righteous forsaken nor his seed begging bread. He will not suffer us to be done wrong.

Rejoice in the Lord and be glad in knowing that He is with you and you are never alone.

STRENGTH BUILDERS

These are some of the things that can help you stay focused while in the midst of your storm.

1. Know that you are whole and are never alone as long as you stay focused on Christ. You must know that you are in Christ and the anointing is in you. Colossians 2:10 says, ***"You are complete in Him which is the head of all principality and powers."***

2. You are more than a conqueror as long as you keep the right attitude and not become selfish or prideful. You can become whatever you want to become and realize that there are no limits to living a victorious life. God may need you to go some place that you would have never thought you would go. Trust God and be available to go when He says go and when you go...go without distractions.

3. Be dedicated. Be devoted. But most importantly, be diligent and available for the things of Christ. Be truthful to yourself. You don't have to pretend by doing things that you don't like to do just to impress somebody else. Don't find yourself doing things just to be accepted by others. Be an original. Know that God loves you just the way you are because He made you. You are beautiful and wonderful because you are made in His image.

4. Know that God has a plan for you and that you must fulfill your destiny. Take one day at a time and learn how to walk in love. Let no one but Jesus sit on the throne of your life. Let no one but

Jesus have control of your life. And let no one but Jesus map out the course for your life. Walk in the path of righteousness (right standing with God).

5. Walk by Faith–Seek God's way of doing things, (God's MOD–Method of Operation) knowing that with God all things are possible.

6. Thank God daily for a life of independence in the things of Christ. *"Trust God with all of your heart and acknowledge Him in all of thy ways and let Him direct your path."* (Proverbs 3:5-6)

7. Get to know who you are in Christ and it will build strong character.

God loves you too much to stand idly by and watch you fall. He'll come to your rescue simply because He made a vow that He would. He's not a man that He should lie, or the son of man that he should have to repent. I live a victorious life because I know Jehova-Jireh is my provider and He is my shield and my strength. As a single woman, I advise you to not let your heart be troubled, nor be afraid. God is our deliverer and He knows what the end result will be. This will only work if you're true to yourself and you're being the best YOU that you can be. Whatever you do, make sure that you always have spiritual insight and that your life is lined up with the Word of God.

PRAYER:

Lord, I thank You because You've met every need in my life. Thank You for keeping me this day and for every blessing You've bestowed upon me. My life is dedicated to You and all grace is abounding towards me. In Jesus' Name, Amen

100

CHAPTER FOURTEEN

ATTITUDE...

Maintaining the Right Attitude When You are in the Midst of a Storm

What is an attitude? It is our true selves in action. It can be your best friend or it can be your worst enemy. Life is an attitude and how you handle it will determine your outcome. How you treat and think about yourself or how you envision your future depends on the attitude (perspective or view) you've developed. Attitude also relates to the position or disposition one takes in life. In short, it's the foundation we build our lives upon as well as the ideas that frame our hopes and dreams. Attitude is a way of thinking and behaving as we experience the many challenges and changes in our lives. A person's attitude is generally derived from what he or she believes and values. However, it's amazing how easily others or circumstances can negatively affect our attitude. It seems to me that when we have bad attitudes, in most cases we've been distracted from the belief that shaped our positive attitude in the first place. Attitude should be the glory of our faith and what we believe. Symbolically as the Church is the glory of Jesus Christ because we were birthed through Christ, the same applies to our attitude; it should be birthed through our faith. I think the reason some people have bad attitudes is because they have no faith.

You cannot serve God unless you do it with the right attitude. Hebrews 11:6 states that it is impossible to please God without faith. I've come to learn through my own life experience that if one lacks faith, he or she will be tossed to and fro and because of the lack of stability. Soon after, usually a victim's mentality (attitude) begins to set in. You may have heard that your attitude determines your altitude and this is so true. Do you like doing things for other people that have bad attitudes all the time? Your attitude is your inward obedience that determines your outward growth. It determines the effectiveness of our relationship with others. It also can affect the attitudes of those around us either positively or negatively. You can't have a bad attitude and have a normal life. Nobody wants to be around someone that consistently has a negative attitude. Your success or failure in life normally hinges on the attitude of the individual because the goal one seeks requires a positive outlook or vision in order to realize it. In order to have a good attitude, you must walk in love. It can turn your problem into a blessing. Never let problems get the best of you. Know that a good or positive attitude doesn't just automatically come. You'll have to work at it by being optimistic and know that God will see you through. A bad attitude is dangerous and can be detrimental, causing harm to those around you. Everything you're going through right now and the things you will have to face is dependent on your attitude. It can have an effect on your health as well. Medical doctors have proven that allowing yourself to be bitter or upset all the time can cause a huge amount of stress and other negative things to happen to your health.

Now you must be honest with yourself. Don't pretend to be something you're not. Always ask God for help when you need it. Matthew 7:7 says, *"Ask and it shall be given, seek and ye shall find, knock and the door will be opened unto you."* Know where your boundaries are and respect others' boundaries as well. Always do your best no matter what you're doing. Do not be so concerned about your needs being met, but spend time making something good happen for somebody else. Now this doesn't mean that you go out and do something good for someone else, just to see what you can get out of it. Now, you know that's the wrong attitude. I heard a person ask another person for a ride home from church before and the other person's response was, "I'm not going that way," and ended up missing an opportunity to make something good happen for that person. Some people are so afraid to get out of their comfort zone to do something for someone else. Remember, you have to keep a humble spirit; don't have a prideful or arrogant spirit. It will cause you to miss out on a lot of blessings and possibly miss out on prosperity and success as well.

Try daily to allow the attitude of Christ to dwell in you. The Scripture admonishes us to allow the mind that was in Christ to be in you, and that mind is to reveal and declare the love of God the Father. So love should be our attitude during both the good and the bad times.

PRAYER

Lord help me to have a right attitude. Help me to think of other people's situations or problems even though I have needs of my own. Lord, the real joy comes from knowing that if I am there to help someone else first; You will be there to help me in my time of need. Now, I thank You Lord for doing it, and I praise You and wait with a "right" attitude. In Jesus' Name, I pray. Amen.

CHAPTER FIFTEEN

Casting Your Cares
Upon the Lord

In trusting God, I knew that I had to cast all my cares on Him. I had to walk in love and not allow bitterness to build a home and set up residence in my heart. I knew God had a plan for me and that all things would work out for my good. Psalm 37:23, *"The steps of a righteous man are ordered by the Lord."* Sometimes it wasn't easy doing the right thing with the right attitude. For example, living holy. I had to pray when others did me wrong. I had to realize that I was working on a relationship with the Lord and that my reward was worth much more than vengeance. Casting away a burden simply means to surrender that burden to a greater authority, which is God.

In order to totally cast your cares upon the Lord, you must allow the Holy Spirit to reveal to you how much love God has stored up for you. God's love is unconditional, and not based on how good you are. You have to be willing to give up something for a deeper walk with God. And usually that something begins with you giving up your will for His will. Even Jesus Christ in the garden of Gethsemane said, *"Father not my will, but thy will be done."* How have we arrived to the place where the creation gives instructions to the Creator? We belong to God and have been created for His good pleasure and purpose and it's important for all to remember that.

There also comes an adjustment with your acceptance of God's will as well. The adjustment begins with one's stewardship over God's possessions, including your life. How can we expect God to entrust more to us when we've not demonstrated that we can be faithful over the little we have now? You can't be elevated to a new level until God knows that He can trust you with where you currently are. Your lack of acceptance can hinder you in many areas. For example, that job promotion that you've been waiting on is dependent on how you treat other people. Well, God is the same way. How do you treat the responsibilities that God has given you? If He told you to do something and you are reluctant in doing it, do you think He is happy with the way you responded to Him? Remember, if God tells you to do something, He will give you the provision to carry that task out. The God I serve is a provider and He will not put more on you than you can bear.

You have to be fully committed to God and fearless in His sight. True faith is exemplified when one knows that God will take care of **all** of their cares. Sometimes you may have to move outside of your safety zone and be placed in uncomfortable situations in order to see victory. Victory doesn't come by you being selfish either. God wants to have full control over your situation. Casting all your cares on the Lord is not limiting Him by saying, "Well Lord you can have this, but I'm not ready to give up this." I know you aren't physically saying this

106

with your mouth, but your actions will show whether or not you're being obedient to the things of God.

It's going to take time for you to get to this place in God, so don't be discouraged. Only God can make the necessary changes that are needed in order to fulfill the plan for your life. We spend too much time looking at our current situations and ourselves. The more you do that, the more that situation will overcome you. Luke 21:34 says, *"Take heed to yourself that you do not get caught up with the cares of this world."*

You're going to have to trust God even when you can't see the light at the end of that tunnel. God didn't promise that He would show us every little intricate detail of how He plans on bringing us out. He did say that *"I am the Way, the Truth, and the Light,"* in John 14:6. When you trust completely in God the way out doesn't seem as important as the one who leads the way. Trusting God means anything is possible, no matter how difficult the problem. Even when doors are closed in your face, He can open them by His power and might. Many of us are always concerned about what others think when we're in vulnerable situations, we must always remember that's the time God is exalted and made strong.

Don't you know that God will not leave you alone? God is standing right there waiting for you to give Him the issues that you're faced with. If God tells you to let go of the very thing that you want to hold on to, will you trust Him enough to release it? No devil in hell can stand in the way of God's divine purpose for your life. It may take a little longer for you to get the promises of God, but due season always comes. God is able to do exceeding and abundant things if you trust in Him. It may hurt, but trust God. You may have to cry; you may even call God and feel like He is not answering you, but trust God. God will deliver you! This is only a test and your promotion is based upon how you finish it. Just know that it is an open book test and all of your answers are found in the word of God. One of the most important things you will have to do in order to get out of that storm you're in is to completely turn all of your cares over to the Lord.

So give it up! Surrender your problems and cares to God. Obtain the solution to the problems that tug at you by saying, "God, it's in your hands. I cast all my cares upon you." Believe it when you say it, and God will work on your behalf.

A PRAYER OF THANKS

Thank You, Father, that the words of my mouth and the meditation of my heart is acceptable in Your sight. Thank You that the eyes of my understanding are enlightened and look only to You for answers to the cares I have given to You. I praise You, Father God, that You are Jehovah-Jireh in my life and that all of my needs are met according to Your riches in glory and no good thing will You withhold from me. I am in the anointed one and the Anointed One is in me. So I can ask boldly anything according to Your will and it shall be because it is Your will to prosper me. It is Your will that I be in good health. Thank You Lord, because You are concerned about everything that concerns me. I walk in the favor of God and the weapons of my warfare are not carnal but mighty through God through the pulling down of strongholds. I thank You, Lord, that You have given me power to tread upon serpents and scorpions and nothing shall by any means harm me or do me wrong. I am more than a conqueror through the anointing that is in me. I am anointed to remove burdens and destroy yokes. No weapon formed against me shall prosper, and I am called according to Your purpose in Jesus Name. Amen

CHAPTER SIXTEEN

Let Go and Let God

How to Release Your Burdens and Pass the Tests of Life

Sometimes you have to give up something in order to gain something better. Worrying and confusion is not of God, so why not exchange it for His peace and joy? God's divine plan for your life has been strategically mapped out for your good. So don't panic when things aren't going as well as you expect them to. Don't start blaming God and others for your hard times. You must learn that life is not all about "Me, Myself and I." Get up from your pity party and move on with your life. Think about this scenario: Say that it's pouring outside. Would you just go and stand in puddles with no protection over your head and no boots on your feet? I hope your response is no. If you don't like the current situation you're in, then you must do something about it. And no, nobody told you that the road would be easy. If they did, then I'm sure you found them to be misleading you by now. II Timothy 3:12 says, *"All that will live Godly, shall suffer persecution."* But guess what? God promised to deliver us from all our hardships.

Although your blessing may be delayed, it's not denied. Let's not ever get so hooked on the things of the world that we can't reap the benefits of the spiritual things. Worldly things are only temporal, but the spiritual things of God are everlasting. Always seek the perfect will of God and know that this is the day that the Lord has made, so rejoice and be glad in it. Your victory may be delayed but if you trust in God it will never be denied. When you believe God to do something in your life, get a vision and believe that it's already done before it comes to pass. When my husband walked out on me, I didn't know how God was going to work things out. Although the answer didn't come when I thought it should, God did answer and again proved that He was attentive to my every need. All I wanted was for the pain and hurt to go away. I wanted to put it all behind me. But, how many of you know that when you have a wound or a sore, it doesn't heal overnight. There is a process in healing; you can't have an operation today and heal tomorrow. Although your healing may be delayed, it will not be denied. In time you will heal. The scar may be there only for a memory and that's the way we have to look at the pain we feel in life. When someone you love has really hurt you, you've got to know that this will pass, too. Put it in God's hands and leave it there. You have the potential of hindering God's plan of deliverance and forcing your break-through to be delayed.

When temptation tries to overtake you, know that God is faithful and He has a way for you to escape. Remember, you can bear all things through Christ who strengthens you, never stop pressing when you're going through. If you stop, how can you tell someone else how to get through? Pressing requires you to deny your flesh, because as long as the flesh is in control you're delaying your victory. Just be patient and continue in faith, not murmuring or complaining and keeping a good attitude.

When something tragic happens to you be still and watch the salvation of the Lord. He's always working things for your benefit if you continue to trust Him. Number one, remember worrying won't change what's already happened. It simply causes unnecessary stress and pain, which eventually causes the natural body to break down. Let it go and let go! Stop dwelling on the problem but instead let His peace dwell in you. The best thing you could do is to focus on a better day coming. God always has a better plan if we trust Him; one far better than we can ask or think. Who has ever loved us like the Lord? No one!

I've not had to work since my job closed down and that was six years ago. All of my needs have been met. Although it didn't come when I expected, yet it was on time. Great is the Lord and greatly to be praised!

Take the limits off of God and yourself and allow Him to do that which you cannot do for yourself. We must let God bless us and look to Him as our total source. God is working when we don't think He is. He's working behind the scenes. Sometimes when we don't see what's happening to us we're quick to say, "It is not working out." That's when we have to walk by faith and not by sight and we must know that God's power is in action and is working for our good. He's working beyond our highest prayer, desires or even our thoughts and dreams. God has given us His promise to help take the limits off of what He can do. He wants us to know that He'll not hold anything back from us if we trust Him. No matter how big our problem seems to be, His grace and resource is much more sufficient than the tasks we're going through.

We need to understand God's word and will for our lives. God is not a God of limits; we are the only ones that are limited. We're the ones to doubt and not believe.

He said in Hebrews 4:12:

My Word is quicker and more powerful and sharper than any two-edged sword, piercing and even dividing asunder of the soul and spirit and of the joints and marrow.

He said that He is the discerner of the thoughts and intents of the heart. God wants us to be equipped to do and perform many good works. God doesn't want us to be ignorant of His will for us. We need to get to know Him in a personal way as a son knows His father. God wants us to be pure in heart. Do not wait for a crisis to happen in your life before you try to get to know Him. It should be a daily thing. Unfortunately, many people never receive all that God has planned for them. Why? It's because of the limitations put on God. When we limit God, it delays our destiny. You must learn how to forget your past failures and stop dwelling on them. Stop talking about how someone treated you wrong and what he or she didn't do for you.

But like Paul said in Philippians 3:13-14,

He counted not himself to have apprehended but this one thing he did, forgetting those things which are behind and reaching for those things which are before, he pressed toward the mark for the prize of the high calling of God in Christ Jesus.

We must take control of our thought life. Why would you want to live thinking about your past, your failures and your hurts? Let God heal you so you can live a victorious life. Having faith in God releases you from a life of limitations. By faith you have been set free and by faith you have been made more than a conqueror. By faith you can receive all the promises of God. When a test comes, be like Paul in James 1:2-4, *"Count it all joy when you fall into diverse temptations, knowing that this is the trying of your faith."* Faith worketh patience and we have to let patience have her perfect work, that we may be made perfect in entirety–wanting nothing.

We must be overcomers and rise above the circumstances. Don't think that you're the only one that has to go through hard times. Everyone experiences something in his or her life; it's just how each chooses to deal with the circumstances. In the midst of a storm, you must know that you're more than a conqueror through God that strengthens you.

I've concluded that there is no failure in God. He's never forsaken me in a desolate land nor left me for the enemy to devour me. He's been a refuge and strong tower. Acknowledge Him in all your ways and He shall direct your paths.

HERE ARE SOME CONSEQUENCES WHEN WE PLACE LIMITS ON GOD:

1. It keeps us from realizing His best.

2. It creates feelings of doubt, worry, and confusion, which leads us to a life of failure and guilt.

3. It promotes self-pride, which is the exalter of the flesh and seeks to destroy all that walk therein. How can a man humble himself to serve God when pride has him thinking he's as wise as God?

4. It destroys our faith because faith works by love, and if we place limits on God we've limited our faith, which can bring into existence the things that we cannot see. Faith grants us access to God's best for your life. It also gives life to the spirit and attitude of man.

THESE ARE SOME OF THE PROMISES WE CAN HAVE IF WE ALLOW GOD TO HAVE HIS WAY AND NOT LIMIT HIM:

1. He promises wisdom to those who ask (James 1:5).

2. He promises forgiveness (1 John 1:9).

3. He promises salvation (Romans 10:13).

4. He promises healing and forgiveness to anyone that is sick (James 5:14-15).

5. He promises deliverance from trouble (Psalms 50:15).

6. He promises freedom from fear and He will give you power, love and a sound mind (2 Timothy 1:7).

7. He promises prosperity (Luke 6:38 and Deuteronomy 28:8).

8. He promises that you should be the head and not the tail (Deuteronomy 28:13).

9. He promises that no weapon formed against you shall prosper (Isaiah 54:17).

10. He promises that with long life He will satisfy us and show us His salvation (Psalm 91:16).

These are just a few of the promises that God gives to those who love Him. If you stand on them by faith, you can access the riches of God's KINGDOM here on earth. When you live by faith, there are no limits to what you can do. In order to overcome the limits in your life, you must live by taking one day at a time and being thankful for each opportunity you have been blessed with.

PRAYER

Father, I thank You for this day. This is the day that You have made and I will rejoice and be glad in it. I thank You Father, that I will take the limits off of You and me. I am free in Jesus' Name. Amen.

CHAPTER SEVENTEEN

Understanding the Principles for Getting out of Any Storm

Sometimes we're too quick to get wrapped up, tied up and tangled up in the cares of this life. When will we realize that the most important thing in life is to love mankind with the love of God? Then and only then will the glorious light of Jesus Christ shine through and we'll draw the world unto Him. The Scripture states that the world would know us by the love we have for each other. It's our birthmark and identifies us even among the unsaved. So let's not hide under a bushel, but instead sit upon a mountaintop for the world to see.

Some of us think that this precious gift was for only us, so we tend to be a little selfish with God's love. We cannot live this life being selfish, because it will cause us to miss the blessing that God has for us. Just as God's love set us free from fear and bondage, why not share God's desire for all to come to repentance (II Peter 3:9) and receive the liberty we now experience. Fear is not an option for those who are in Christ, because perfect love casts out all fear. Fear torments and seeks to kill you.

Fear eventually leads to failure; you must let go of whatever is making you fearful. God is your deliverer and His presence alone drives out fear. Always do the best with what you have and don't worry about the things you can't control. Just get busy controlling the things that God's entrusted to you and soon you'll begin to see a harvest. There's no place in this world that's trouble-free. Anything in life worth having will cost you something. Yes, salvation is free to us, yet it cost God the life of His beloved Son. We can't worry about the small things that come up in our lives. Never let temporary setbacks cause you to become discouraged and quit; always set your goals high and always aim to obtain them. Don't be so quick to doubt things; know that doubt is an obstacle, but faith sees the way. Doubt sees the darkest night, but faith sees a brighter day. God always has great things for them that have faith in Him. Hebrews 11:6 says, *"God is a rewarder to those that diligently seek Him."* Faith will refuse to see anything that is contrary to what God's Word says. It doesn't look at the problem or the condition that you're in; it only looks at the promises that God has stored up for us.

Sometimes, we stay in the storm so long because we feel like it is too much to bear. We start attending pity parties and the only ones that seem to show up are people just like us. We seem to enjoy talking about our problems and seem to glory in them as well. I heard a joke one time about a woman testifying in church. She got so caught up in what the devil was doing to her that she started saying, "The devil has been riding my back all week. The devil has been giving me a hard time; that old devil is something, bless his holy name." The point? When you start giving the devil so much credit, you will forget about what God has done for you, because there is nothing holy about the devil.

120

Impatience is a tool that will cost you much. Some people are so impatient that they want everything right now. They will pray, "Lord I need You and I need You right now!" And that's where we make most of our mistakes. It puts unnecessary pressure on you and those around you. How can the creation place demands on the Creator? We must learn how to just trust, believe and let go. Here's the life lesson I've learned; whatever will be, will be; the future is not something we need to see. Only walk by faith and see yourself victorious.

"Faith is the substance of things hoped for and the evidence of things not seen." (Hebrews 11:1). Don't wait until you can figure out the problem before you see your way out. Remember that life is dependent on the choices that you make. God is so good that He allows us to make decisions. So expect something good to happen to you every day, and if it doesn't, you shouldn't start making excuses. We must learn that excuses hinder our progress. Always be ready for opportunities when they come knocking on your door. Don't put off for tomorrow what you can do today. If success does not work the first time, change how you are doing things and try it another way. You must go forward and be open to whatever adjustments God wants us to make. Know who you are in Christ; know that you are precious and wonderfully made, because God does not make junk. That's what keeps me going in my hard times. I know that God loves me in spite of what anyone else may have felt. Don't get caught up with people and the bondage they try placing on you. If you do they'll control you. Don't ever give anyone the authority to control your life. I tell you God is in control of my life. He gave me life and He said I could have it more abundantly. This alone should motivate you to do your best in whatever you are doing. Always be willing to go a little farther. Don't wait to fail or be abused by others.

You'll find often that life responds to our outlook. So go ahead and have high expectations. Learn to love everyone and the things you allow to happen in your life will be good.

PRAYER

Father, I thank You for wisdom to do the things that will make a change in my life for my good. Thank You for being Jehovah-Jireh, my provider. Amen

CHAPTER EIGHTEEN

Living a Life of Diligence

Who Is Doing The Talking?

Know When to Shut-up and Let God Speak On Your Behalf.

Exodus 15:26 says that,

If thou will diligently hearken to the voice of the Lord and do that which is right in His sight, and give ear to His commandment and keep His statutes, He will not put diseases upon thee; For He is the Lord that healeth thee.

"If we are diligent in the things of God, we can possess the good of the land." (Deuteronomy 6:17) If you remain diligent, every place the soles of your feet touch shall be blessed and no evil shall overtake you. Serving the Lord has its privileges. By proclaiming His Word and holding fast to His truths, God will send the latter rain into your dry places and you shall know no lack. I know it might not look like things are going to change on your behalf, but when it's your time; it's your

time. I'm sure you have heard that whatever God has for you, it is for you. You've got to believe that good things just don't happen to people. Somewhere along the way they sowed seeds and what you're seeing are the fruits of those seeds. In that same respect, you might be wondering why it looks as if that person that isn't serving the Lord or the one that is always doing you wrong is always excelling in life. It's only for a season. The sun shines on the just and the unjust, but if they're not diligent in their relationship with God soon the wealth they've acquired will be transferred to the righteous. Don't be alarmed the tables will turn and God will release a blessing that you won't have room enough to receive. Why will he do it? God is kind, just and full of compassion. His mercies are tender and new every day. Remain committed to pleasing Him and you too will experience the sure mercies of David.

Hearken unto the voice of God and you shall be blessed in the city. You shall be blessed in the fields and blessed in your body. Every time you walk out the door and come back home, blessings will be following you and waiting on your return. You've got a special delivery at the other end of your diligence, but the question is...will you be there to sign for the package? How many times have you canceled out blessings because you were too quick to give up? When you completely trust in the Lord, your enemies come in one way, but before you know it God has spoken on your behalf and said, "Stop, no more."

With diligence, you have to know when to allow God to do the talking for you. You have to know when you need to shut up your physical mouth and let God work it out on your behalf. He'll be your lawyer in the courtroom. And guess what...He's never lost a case. So you may be saying, "Marjorie, when am I supposed to speak on my behalf?"

The only time that you should open your mouth on the situation is through confessions or when you know it is God telling you to speak. You have so much power through your confessions unto the Lord. Once you start a lifestyle of prayer and confession, you'll notice that when you have to face that struggle or that uneasy situation, God will speak up when you speak out. Remember, whatever you put in must come out of you. Isn't it about time you let God do the talking?

Here's what the Lord will do for you, based upon your diligence. *He shall command the blessings upon you in your storehouses and in all that you put your hand to.* (Deuteronomy 28: 1-14). He shall bless me in the land which the Lord thy God has given to you. We are a holy people established by God and if we keep His commandments and walk in His ways, all the people of the earth shall see that we are called by the name of the Lord. The Lord shall make us plenteous in goods and in the fruit of our body and in everything we plan to have prosperity in. The Lord shall open unto us His good treasures and bless all the works of our hands. We shall lend and not borrow because the Lord shall make us the head and not the tail. *"We shall be above only and not beneath"* (Proverbs 10:4). *"The hand of the diligent shall rule and His substance is precious"* (Proverbs 21:5). The thoughts of the diligent tend only to plenteous. If we will be diligent in not only hearing the Word of God but also doing what it says, He will make an everlasting covenant with us. Whatever you do, do it with all diligence, whether it is exalting the Lord, giving your tithes and offerings, working in the ministry or teaching; do it with the right motivation. God made a promise to Abraham and to us because we are of Abraham's seed. He said that He would bless us and multiply us. We know that *"God is a rewarder of them that diligently seek*

Him" (Hebrew 11:6). When we give our all and do everything that God has commanded us to do, we shall never fall. So look for such things.

Be diligent so you may be found of Him in peace without spot, and blameless. Grow in grace and in the knowledge of Jesus Christ, the anointed one and His anointing.

(II Peter 3: 14-18)

PRAYER

Lord, let Your love abound more and more in knowledge and in all judgment. Lord, only approve of those things that are excellent in Your sight. Allow me to be sincere in the things I do and to not get offended until the day of Your return. Lord, fill me with the fruits of righteousness unto the glory and praise of God. Deal bountifully with Your servant that I may live and keep Your Word. Open my eyes so I can behold Your wondrous things. Hide not Your commandments from me and quicken me according to Your Word. Teach me Your statutes and make me understand the way of Your commandments, so I shall talk of Your wondrous works without fear or shame. Give me understanding in my heart and I shall keep it. I shall observe it and incline my whole heart unto Your testimonies. Don't allow covetousness or vanity anywhere near my dwelling place. Establish Your Word unto me and let Your mercies come to me. Let Your kindness and Your peace overshadow me forever. Amen

THERE MAY BE MANY QUESTIONS ABOUT HOW TO GET THROUGH HARD TIMES.

1. What do you do when you have been abandoned?

2. How do you raise five children without any help from the system?

3. How do you keep your right mind, without losing it?

The answer to all these questions is...You MUST learn how to trust God! Until I learned how to trust God, I could not answer these questions.

I want to talk to you about Proverbs 3:5-6,

Trust in the Lord with all Your heart and lean not to your own understanding, in all Your ways acknowledge Him and He will direct your path.

This is the greatest thing to do while in His presence. I want to talk to you about How to trust God, why to trust God and the benefits of trusting God.

Let's define trust...
     Trust means protection.
     Trust means provider.
     Trust means peace.

God is all of these things and more. He's our protection. He's our provider. He's our Peace, but you still may ask...

How do I trust God?

You must trust Him with your WHOLE heart. The heart is the most important part of your being. It is where the essence of life flows; your emotion, your affection.

Why trust God?

He is our protection. He protects us like we protect small children when someone is trying to hurt them. He provides for us the same way we feed and clothe them, making sure all of their needs are met. God only wants the best for us. We know that He will never leave us nor forsake us as long as we let Him. We must have absolute trust in Him and be unshaken. We must know that God will give us the strength to succeed in every task that comes against us. He is our refuge and our high tower, a strong hold in times of trouble. God is concerned about everything that concerns us. Isaiah 26:3 says, *"He will keep us in perfect peace if we keep our mind on Him."* Psalm 138:8 says, *"The Lord will perfect that which concerneth me."*

We must be confident in what Romans 4:21 says, "being fully persuaded that what He promised He is able to also perform it." We must be steadfast, unmovable, and always choose to walk in love; keeping the right attitude ,knowing that God will make all grace abound toward us, and we will have all sufficiency in everything.

We must settle in our hearts that God loves us and He wants the best for us. He is the Shepherd of our souls. We must believe Isaiah 54:17: *"No weapon that is formed against us shall prosper."*

We must trust Psalm 91:10-11 which says,

No evil shall befall me, neither shall any plague come near my dwelling place. For God shall give His angels charge over me to keep me in all my ways.

And verse 16 which says, *"With long life will He satisfy me and show me His salvation."*

One thing we must know for sure is that God cares for us no matter what we may be going through. You've got to know that He knows your circumstances; He knows your thoughts. He said come unto me all that labor and are heavy laden; He said He will give you rest (Matthew 11:28).

God wants us to trust and rest in Him. So many times we try to fix things ourselves by trying this and by trying that. These struggles are the cares of this life and they're not the plan of God. God wants to bear our burdens.

In Matthew 11:29-30, Jesus tells us,

Take my yoke upon you and learn from me, for I am meek and lowly in heart, and ye shall find rest unto your souls. He said, "My yoke is easy and My burden is light."

You see, He wants to give us peace and doesn't want our hearts to be troubled; neither does He want us to be afraid. Through His spirit He offers us inner peace and strength.

There have been times in my life when I wondered if God cared about the fiery tests I was going through. I had to re-focus and remind myself that this is just a test. I realized that I would never have a testimony without a test. You have to know that it is a test and you're not alone in it. Even if it feels like no one else is there, or no one else cares. God is there for you. When we put our trust in God we don't need to get all frustrated over things that happen.

Principles for standing in the midst of the storm:

- Pray always.
- Praise and worship Him.
- Daily confess God's Word.
- Keep the right attitude.
- Stay focused.
- Do not be weary.
- Do not be double-minded.
- Do not murmur and complain.
- Don't be a gossiper or judgmental.
- Always be thankful.

Always pray that the will of God be done over your life and those with whom you come in contact. *"Call those things that be not as though they were"* (Romans 4:17). When praising God, tell Him how much you love Him and sing songs that will build you up. Look up all the promises that God says we can have and stand on every one of them. God is true to His Word.

After you have been through the storm, your testimony will be a blessing to someone else that might be going through those same storms. Remember if God did it for me, He can do the same for you.

DO YOU KNOW HIM?

Have you had a born-again experience with the Lord and Savior, Jesus Christ? Has He changed you from inside out? Do you know Him in the power of His might? If you don't know God in the power of His might, I encourage you to please get to know Him personally. You can read about what He's done for someone else, but the most important thing is getting to know what He can do for you. Some people have no clue about who my Lord and Savior Jesus Christ is. They know nothing about the wonder-working power of God. They may say, "Yeah, I know Him," but their actions will show just how much they know about Him. When you begin to talk about the mighty works of God and how He heals, delivers, and sets free. For example, the disciples were with Jesus and saw the miracles that He did; they listened to His words and even they did not have a clue of who Jesus really was.

How do I know? If they had truly known who He really was, they wouldn't have panicked when they were in the midst of the storm in the middle of the sea. The winds got rough and the ship really began to rock. The first thing they thought was that they were going to drown; they forgot Jesus was on board the ship.

That's why I say, if they really had known whom Jesus was they wouldn't have panicked. They would have known that it was impossible for them to perish. When they panicked, they woke Him up, saying, **"Careth not that we perish?" Jesus just spoke to the storm and said, "Peace, be still!"** So if you are in the midst of a storm, whether it is like theirs or not, just know that He can speak to your storms, too!

My friend, get to know Him so He can set you free. Isaiah 54:17 says, **"No weapon that is formed against**

131

you shall prosper." Psalm 91:7 says, *"A thousand shall fall at thy side and ten thousand at thy right hand, but it shall not come near thee."* These promises are only for those that have given their lives over to the most high God. These are the fringe benefits to those who have made Jesus Christ their Lord and Savior. When you get to know Him you'll never walk , even when you feel all hope is gone. So be strong, my friend, and walk on through the storm. Whatever is holding you in the midst of your storm, you must let it go. Stop the madness; turn it loose. Be free! Nothing in life is more important than being free and living a victorious life. Let the peace of God rest, rule and abide in your heart. So that you can rejoice and be glad that you can rest at night. Let the joy of the Lord be your strength. Delight yourself in the Lord and He will give you the desires of your heart. Know that you're more than a conqueror. I've been there, but thanks be unto God that I am triumphant now. I have passed the tests and fiery trials. May God bless you with all wisdom and knowledge concerning the mysteries of His Kingdom. All things are possible with God! So, please, please get to know Him. If you don't know Him, may I take this time to help lead you in prayer to get to know Him? Please pray this prayer and allow Him to come into your life and heart and you too shall live the abundant life.

PRAYER OF SALVATION

Dear Heavenly Father, I come to You in the Name of Jesus Christ. You said that anyone that comes to You, You will in no way cast out. So Father, I come to You asking You to forgive me of all my sins, wash me and make me whole. I confess with my mouth that I am a sinner. I believe in my heart that Jesus Christ is the Son of God and He

*died and rose again for my sins. I ask You to
please save me. Come into my heart and show me
how to live for You. Thank You, dear Lord, for
forgiving me and saving me. In Jesus' Name I
pray. Amen.*

CHAPTER NINETEEN

How to Live in Victory and Enjoy the Good Life

First, you must maintain standards. Don't just let anyone come in and invade your life. You must learn how to prioritize the most important things in your life and be watchful of those things that are not as important.

Maintain a life that pleases God and that leads to your purpose. A purpose-driven life is one that fulfills the individual completely both spiritually and naturally. Yes God will give you the desires of your heart and will satisfy your thirst. Your days should be like Heaven on Earth; a life of freedom. Live each day with love. Love your neighbor as thyself. Be the best that you can be and do unto others as you would want them to do unto you. Don't stay stuck in your past. Always look forward to your future and be happy. Be free and let not your heart be troubled. Don't allow yourself to become stressed out. Always find time to rest and don't allow the pressures of this life to get you down.

Maybe some of you are asking yourselves and wondering how did I became so blessed from sleeping on the floor to moving into a new $295,000. home, paid for in cash.

God took a bad situation and turned it around for my good. My father was stricken with a stroke and was hospitalized. The doctor said he wouldn't live and even if he did, he would only live three days. But, as we all know, life is not in man's hands, my father lived almost six months after the stroke.

As a result of me and my sisters not being able to take care of him at home, we had to put him in a nursing home that could provide total assisted living care. He was paralyzed on one side; this situation became a nightmare. He was neglected so badly that his condition was unbearable and unbelievable. God allowed us to bring a lawsuit against that nursing home. God showed us so much favor that we were able to settle the case out of court for an undisclosed amount.

Even in the storm of losing a loved one, God showed us His blessings in the financial realm. I thank God that my father's death wasn't in vain, though it looked like a bad situation, but God worked it out for my good. God said all good and perfect gifts come from Him.

When all this was happening, I wondered why my father suffered so much. One night I was looking at what a blessing I received from all this and God reminded me of how He suffered and how He hung, bled and died so that I may have eternal life.

After that, I began to thank Him, for now I know that sometimes life may not seem fair, but God can take a bad situation and turn it around for our good, when our trust is in Him!

136

Special Thanks:

To my two sisters Helen Stewart and Nell Cook and their husbands Jake and Ezell. Thank you Helen, for all of the times I needed you for loans. Thank you for all you and Nell have done for my children and me. I would like to thank my nieces and nephews also: Jarhunda Stewart, Tonya, Kevin and Keith Cook. I love you all. May God bless you for whatever you did for me in times of my storms.

I thank God for my Aunt Annie and her long life. I thank God that after so many years of being apart, He has allowed us to reunite for a time such as this. Love always!

I would like to give thanks to my brother-in-law and sister-in-law Mr. & Mrs. John and Bobbie Simon. You were always there for me. You were my "Ace in the hole." You were my banker, my encouragers, and my friends. Thanks for standing by me. No matter what storm came, you hung in there with me. I would like to thank my nieces, Terea, Lashea and Tarsha for all the lovely cards and the beautiful flowers of encouragement that I received from you during my times of testing. Love always and forever.

To my dear sister-in-law Vera M. Gaskins, you have not been like a sister-in-law, you have been like my own sister. Thanks for being one that led me to Christ. With your loving kindness toward me, you knew the storm that I was going through. You knew the peace that I needed so badly. You showed me that the peace was not in your brother, but it was in Christ. I love you, I feel indebted to you for help showing me how to surrender and cast my cares upon the Lord. Vera, I know you love me. You have proven your love to me over and over many times. I know you know I love you. You can count on me no matter what it may be! Love you, girl.

To my best girlfriend, Sister Barbara Robinson: you are the one that God blessed us to become like blood sisters. You were there for us all of the time, with your support, your love, and your money. You always found time to assist us in the midst of my storm. God bonded us together as a spiritual family. Love you always.

To my dear sister, Mary O'Neil, my friend! Thank you for being my prayer warrior. You were the one who prayed for my children and me all of the time. It was you that kept me from getting weary many times. You continued to keep my arms lifted up and you interceded for my strength. I want you to know, that I shall never forget your labor of love. You have my love and prayer always.

To my friend, my buddy, and my prayer partner, Sister Cora Anderson: you have been there for us with your love, your encouragement, and your money. My children highly respect you and love you, too. Brother Frank Anderson, thank you for being a great man of God and allowing your wife to share her life with us. God bless you all. There will always be a special place in my heart for you all. Much love. *Since I wrote this book, my dear friend has passed on to a better life. I write this in loving memory of all the good times we've had.*

To Ms. Ivell, the one who has been like a mother to my children and me. You have always treated us like we were your very own. I know your daughters Daisy and Lizzy know that I was that other daughter that you did not birth, but was just as dear to you. They respected that and loved me the same. You all will always be a part of my family. I love you, and your family. May God bless you and if you ever need me, I am only a phone call away. Your other daughter, Marjorie. *Since I wrote this book, my dear friend has passed on to a better life. I write this in loving memory of all the good times we've had.*

To my good friends, Norma Robinson and Sister Catheryn Jackson. Thank you, girls, for the good times we shared together. Love you. You know where you are in my heart.

To my former church family, Gospel Temple, I would like to say thank you all for the twenty-eight years I served with you. Thank everyone for the part you played in my life and for helping me through the storms I was in. You were there in my good times and my bad times. I shall never forget you all and I shall always respect and remember the late Dr. Herd Seals. To Mother Bessie Seals, (the pastor's wife) for encouraging me with the words, "Do not be weary in well doing, for due season will come." I thank you, Mother Seals; I am living in that season now and it is good, very good. Prayerfully yours, and I'll love you always.

To my good friend, Odessa Ameys, I want to thank you very much for all of the times I have shared my dreams with you and how many times I have eaten your good cooking. You are very special to me. Love always, your sister. *Since I wrote this book, my dear friend has passed on to a better life. I write this in loving memory of all the good times we've had.*

I would like to take the time to thank and give honor and respect to the Godparents of my five children. They were a great blessing to me while I was in the midst of my storms. To the late mother Frances Dowdell, who was the Godparent of my first-born Wardell, she loved him with all her heart.

To Mr. & Mrs. L. B. and Ann Coney, the special Godparents of my first daughter, Laurie Ann; you were very good Godparents to her. Thank you for loving her dearly and for all the help and support you gave me with her.

To Mr. & Mrs. Nathaniel and Cindy Shaw, thanks for being the special Godparents of my second daughter, Dolores, you were very good to her. Thanks for your advice and your love.

To Mr. & Mrs. James and Sue Patterson, the special Godparents of my baby boy, Don. You all have been such a blessing to him. When he was born, Sue, you were not married to Brother Patterson, but thank you for all of the lavish gifts you showered him with. After you were married, Brother Patterson, you joined in and became a great inspiration in Don's life. Thank ya'll (come to see us). Love you very much.

To Mr. & Mrs. Freeman & Lillian Finch, the special Godparents of my baby girl Ronda. You all were such a blessing. Thanks for treating her like she was your very own. Thanks for supplying all of her "special occasion" clothing when she was small. You all have been a very great blessing in my life. I thank you for all of your acts of love while we were in the midst of our storm. Love you dearly.

I would like to honor two special friends that were on my job and who were like brothers to me. First, I would like to thank Paul Blake, for your love and your advice and just for being there for me after my separation and divorce. Thanks for allowing me to unload my burdens on you. You were always willing and patient to listen to me. I felt your concern. Thanks again, Paul, for your ear to listen and your understanding heart. There will always be a bond in my heart for you. Love you.

Mr. Ira Schrub: thank you Ira, for being that big brother with a big heart and big shoulders for me to lean on. You were always there for me trying to advise me on what I needed to do to get out of this messy storm I was in. I want to thank your wife Cynthia for allowing you to share your wisdom and time with me. I just want you all to know the storm is over in my life. Thanks again for your support and thanks for being in my life. God bless you. I love you.

To all of my spiritual children: I thank God for blessing me to have spiritual children just as dear to me as my natural children.

WHO DO MEN SAY THAT I AM?

I thought it only befitting that my natural children and two of my closest friends have words to say. This is the unedited version of our relationship. I Love You All...Ma

WARDELL SIMON, JR.
(First-born child/son)

I would like to thank the "Lord Jesus Christ " for a mother that just wouldn't give up on me.

My mother is an inspiration, and I admire her courage and also her walk with the Lord. She has been through numerous "Storms" on my behalf, as well as her own. I truly believe that Mom has a "special anointing" on her life and that anointing is passed on to all that come in contact with her.

Momma, I want you to know: I Love you! And I'm sorry for all those times I broke your heart. Thank you for forgiving me. Thank you for standing in the gap for me when things looked hopeless.

Things are looking a lot better now; and the Lord has forgiven me also. He has saved me and filled me with the

Holy Ghost and redeemed my life from destruction.

Your prayers were heard; those many nights you paced the floor and wondered would I ever CHANGE? Those prayers weren't in vain and they didn't fall on deaf ears.

The Lord heard each prayer you prayed! And He wants you to know: THE BEST IS YET TO COME! *"He's pleased with your faithfulness,"* and He is a rewarder of those who diligently seek him.(Hebrew 11: 6)

So no matter how rough the storms of life get, know that the Lord is there to step in and say: *"Peace, be still."*

Mom, I wish you God's blessings upon every endeavor you challenge. I know you are empowered to prosper, and I am glad I'm an heir. I love you.

Your first seed... is growing.
Jr.

LAURIE ANN SIMON
(Second child, first-born daughter)

To my mother; the one who raised me to the best of her ability. I now realize today that I contributed a lot toward the storms my mother went through. She was always there for me. No matter what I did she never turned her back on me. I do thank you, Mom. Foremost, I thank God for being in your life because without Him you would not have made it.

Love you,
Your daughter, Laurie

DOLORES SIMON-BURGESS
(Third child, second-born daughter)

I guess you could say that I'm the child who takes after my mother the most. Two of my siblings look like her and the rest of us take after my father. I would say I'm the one who really takes after her; I think my siblings would all agree. I have her mothering ways, her strength (to a certain point) and her wisdom. Although I'm not as spiritual as she and I'm not where I need to be or where she would like me to be, but we are alike in so many ways. When I was told that my mother was writing a book about her legacy it got me to thinking about my own life and how this would be her permanent mark in this world and how it will live on. I'm glad that this was placed in her heart to encourage others.

There are so many things to say about this wonderful person who was given to me. I must have been pretty special to the Man up above for him to place her in my life. I can truly say her life has been a journey. With her divorce and all of the responsibilities placed on her she decided that she could make it. I can honestly say that there have been tough times and not once did my mother give up. She could have walked out on the mortgage, car note, kids, and a bunch of other bills, but she was determined to stand still and let God do His work in her life. My mother is the strongest person that I know. I try to model myself after her in that way, but due to the other half that completes me it makes it impossible. You see, on my father's side they are aggressive, but very sensitive. We will cry at the drop of a hat and are often called the crying Simons. But, she has the strength to move mountains; I'd hate to wonder that if she didn't place God first in her life where would we be.

145

As for my two wonderful children they have nothing but great things to say about Ma or Gramma as they call her. Not only has she been a grandmother, but a mother figure as well in their lives. I, as well as my husband and children, are so grateful to have someone so magnificent in our lives. We, as well as her, have our days and when that's done and over with, everything is still the same. JauQuin and Kharia know that they have a special place in her heart and she would do anything, and I mean anything, for them. As would I for her. I know sometimes she may think that we are selfish and into our own lives, but she knows that I'm only trying to be that mother that she is to me. I'm sure I could go on and on, but I'm sure that I have expressed my thoughts of my mother to everyone.

Love always,
"Lois"

DON ERIC SIMON
(Fourth-born child, second son)

There really is no place to start when I talk about my mother. I can sum her up with two words...Strong Tower. Ever since I can remember, I've noticed no other woman in my life to endure what she has and still remain standing after every storm. Sure she was whipped, beaten, talked about, and mistreated, but that was all a part of the struggle to become the "Loosed Woman" she is today. She has been my mother and my father and ﹃etimes my closest friend.

﹃hat this book will be a complete success
ᵕo much healing power in it for every
ᵕd every man with a struggle. God is
ᵕer in every chapter and even though

146

there is so much in this book, there still is a lot to be uncovered in her presence. Mom, thank you for being my life giver and thank you for allowing me to live!!!

Mom always talks about how her children watch her reactions to certain situations that may arise in her and their lives. The reason, I believe, is because we look for some type of validation or approval before we make a concrete decision. A lot of people that she has counseled want to know if they are making the right decisions, or at least would like to get her opinion on the matter. It's very rare that she will give you an answer that will sway you left or right. She wants you to be responsible for your actions and not do something simply because she suggested it. This is all a part of growing up and being your own person with your own storms to conquer.

I love you and I wish you the best and thank you for listening to me and putting "some" of your testimony on paper. I later found out that this is only a little of what you went through, but as you said, some things are best left unspoken.

You are my friend...Don

RONDA R. DARITY
(Fifth-born child, third daughter, the baby and last of the siblings)

The best teachers are those who lead by example and my mother has done just that. Mom has influenced my life tremendously by being a true woman of faith. When I was growing up she didn't just sit down with me and verbally teach me the Bible or the Word of God, but mo importantly she showed me how to serve God the l way she knew how. She made sure that we went to church every Sunday, which taught me how to reverence God. She also made sure that we respected adults and our elders by not talking back to them; and by saying "Yes ma'am" and "Yes sir." Those are things that still stick with me today. My mom has also taught me how to pray and was there to help me with my nightly prayers; and when I was too little to memorize them by myself, she got down there on her knees and said them with me until I could memorize them by myself. She has also shown me how to be a true giver and a sower. As a child, I would see her give to people even if it was her last. If they needed something, she would give it and would believe God to meet her own needs.

My mother always wanted us to have the best of things in life. She worked hard for us to have them too. We never went a birthday or Christmas without a gift; never a night to bed without a meal and never a school year without new school clothes. She also made sure that we were always clean and well dressed. Being a single mother of five, that in itself is an accomplishment. She has showed me how to be strong in the midst of hard times. When our father left her, and we stood there on the porch to watch him leave, she didn't want us to cry. She wanted us to know that with the help of God everything was going to be all right. And it was. I don't know where or how our lives would have turned out if it weren't for my mom's faith in God. Life hasn't always been easy for her, and at times I even made it difficult for her. I'm glad to ⸱ that through it all, she has learned how to trust God ⸱idst of the storm. This has changed my life ⸱e learned how to love the Lord and trust ⸱ver the years I have learned so much I am grateful for. I am learning each the knowledge and the wisdom that she has, so that one day I may be able to impart some of that wisdom and knowledge into my own children's lives. I just want to say thank you, Mom, for never giving up on us because your love and faith in God has made a tremendous impact in my life and the lives of others.

Love Always,
Your Youngest Daughter, Ronda

WORDS FROM CLOSE FRIENDS:

BARBARA ROBINSON

The Lord saw a need for a good friend in my life, and he sent Sister Marjorie. It has been a spiritually, uplifting experience to know her.

We met at Gospel Temple COGIC around 1974. We both sat on the same pew. Before long we became the best of friends. Through the years our friendship has continued to blossom. Sister Marjorie has blessed my life with her strong faith in God. She always has words to strengthen and encourage in whatever you are going through. We have been through many storms, but her faith in God has never wavered.

Sister Marjorie is a caring and giving person, and the Lord has blessed her for her faithfulness.

Your Sister in the Lord and dearest Friend,
Sister Barbara Robinson

Evangelist Miriam D. Hughes

I have known Marjorie Simon for the past five years. She is a very inspirational, dedicated, loving person whose primary concern is following the path on which God leads her. She is sold out to God. Therefore, no matter where God leads her, she will follow. Marjorie never frowns upon life's experiences nor does she take anything for granted. Marjorie's kind and warm smile always seems to state that she has a testimony for whatever the situation. Her experiences have taught her how to trust and lean on God's everlasting arm. She has always been such a good friend and my spiritual support. No matter what! Neither the time of day nor the hour when you call matters; she will respond. May God bless this humble worker who has taken this calling to share her life's experiences as You, Father, have instructed her. May her words touch the hearts of everyone who reads her life story with encouragement, letting them know that God IS! In closing, Psalm 90 states, *"God will bless in success the works of your hands."* Continue in God's will, obedience, love, and works. Prosper always.

Your friend and Sister-in-Christ,
Evangelist Miriam D. Hughes